FERRO-CEMENT BOAT CONSTRUCTION

Ferro-Cement
Boat Construction

By

Jack R. Whitener

Cornell Maritime Press, Inc.

Cambridge   1971   *Maryland*

ISBN 0–87033–140–X

Library of Congress Catalog Card Number: 76-124468

Printed in the United States of America

Second Printing, January 1973

To

Herb and Jean Metcalf

who helped when it was most needed, and

To

Tom Sharp

who just listened during the early days when I first became interested in ferro-cement boats

CONTENTS

ACKNOWLEDGMENTS

I wish to thank the following firms, institutes, schools, and individuals for their invaluable help and information that contributed to the compilation of this book:

Kaiser Cement & Gypsum Corporation, Mr. Robert R. Beck, Permanente, California

Mr. Lee Byran (Kaiser Publications, Oakland, California)

American Concrete Institute, Mr. William A. Maples, Detroit, Michigan

Portland Cement Association, Mr. J. H. Walker, Skokie, Illinois

Expanded Shale, Clay and Slate Institute, Mr. Frank G. Erskine, Washington, D.C.

Eagle-Picher Industries, Mr. L. T. Montant, Jr., Ohio

The Master Builders Co., Mr. H. L. McFalls, Oakland, California

Civil Engineering & Public Works Review, Mr. V. J. Wilmoth, London, England

Concrete Publications, Limited, Mr. T. Sheridan, London, England

Basalt Rock Company, Mr. Paul R. Hennessey, Jr., Napa, California

Redwood Ferro-Crete, Mr. R. E. Graham, Redwood City, California

Engineering School, Trinity College, Dublin 2, Ireland:
    Mr. J. G. Byrne, Computer Science Dept.
    Mr. W. Wright, Prof. of Engineering
    Mr. R. W. Kirwan, Lecturer, Eng. School
    Mr. L. D. G. Collen, Lecturer, Eng. School

Metal Lath Manufacturers Association, Cleveland, Ohio

Perlite Institute, New York, New York

Robert J. Westervelt, R. J. Westervelt & Associates, Washington, D.C.

Mr. K. H. Brittain, Mr. A. L. Edge, The Cement Marketing Co., Ltd., Portland House, London S.W. 1., England

Lloyds Register of Shipping, London, E.C. 3, England

British Standards Institution, 2 Park Street, London, W. 1., England

Dr. Fred Kagy, Industrial Arts Dept., Illinois State Normal University, Illinois

Cornell Maritime Press, Inc., Mr. Robert F. Cornell, Cambridge, Maryland

North American Ferro-Cement Marine Association, Inc., 1959 Old Middlefield Road, Mountain View, California 94040

Pictures of "open-mold method" are used with permission of Redwood Ferro-Cement and Mr. R. H. Muenzer, Mountain View, California.

Pictures of hull plastering, finishing, curing and hull stiffeners are used with permission of Mr. Austin L. Edge, Technical Department, Cement Marketing Company, Ltd., London, England.

J. R. W.

FOREWORD

The author has done extensive research on methods of ferro-cement yacht construction and on its advantages and disadvantages. The information contained in this publication is concise and to the point and fills a need long felt by the people who are contemplating construction of ferro-cement yachts.

If the worth of a book is judged by the knowledge contained and easily made available to the reader, then this volume will stand as the book most responsible for fine boats and yachts made of ferro-cement.

Richard H. Muenzer

PREFACE

This book has been written to help those readers who have not been acquainted with the "hidden things" that are so often necessary when undertaking a construction project. In this case we are talking about building a boat from the very first time it becomes a goal in the builder's mind.

It is often said that the simple things are the most difficult to execute. This may be true if it is something new. However, with a bit of elementary knowledge it becomes simple and easy to build. My interest has been in anything that will float, and the most challenging aspect is its construction.

This was the case when I read an article about ferro-cement boats. Without knowing a thing, I dashed out and investigated. This time I had a place to work and it was obvious that the most rudimentary tools would be sufficient. The iron framework took shape and busy weekends followed.

Hidden problems kept popping up in the form of how to support the boat prior to applying cement, how to launch it properly, and whether I had used the correct mixture of sand and cement. Well, *Captain Sinclair* floated—that was about all. She oversteered, was slow, and consumed an inordinate amount of fuel when used for fishing. The only sizable outboard that I could get was a very old 5-horse motor with a small 3-horse motor to go along as a spare. My crew, who were *sans* boat, volunteered to take the flattie out to the middle of Choctawhatchee Bay. Later that evening, when they returned, the smallest member exclaimed: "Gee, it rode like a Cadillac out there!" They had encountered 3–4-foot waves on that windy day in April, so there was at least one good feature about my first ferro-cement flattie.

My good friend Charlie Law, who helped apply and mix a large amount of cement, commented that our learning curve was acquired the hard way. In my estimation, there was a huge loss of precious weekend time. That lesson has been with me ever since and was one of the main reasons for writing this book. Another is to pass on as much information as possible to the prospective builder so that he can do it right the first time—*and* to help him get started on the right track and have the boat waterborne within the shortest building time.

Jack R. Whitener

FERRO-CEMENT BOAT CONSTRUCTION

I

TOOLS AND EQUIPMENT

Plaster/Mortar Mixer

The plaster/mortar cement mixer is an item of paramount importance, a must for ferro-cement. See Fig. 1-1. It is designed to thoroughly mix water, cement, aggregates, and pozzolans into one dry homogeneous mass. This is accomplished by a horizontal blade, with a rotating mixing action, as opposed to the vertical revolving drum cement mixer. There are many different sizes, models and prices.

In England the vertical tilting drum mixer has been used successfully for some years. The American horizontal rotating blade plaster/mortar mixer is not available in England. The horizontal rotating blade mixer produces a drier mix than the vertical drum mixer.

Prices on mixers vary, I contacted several construction equipment dealers and asked for brochures and prices on mixers. The brochures arrived with the prices written in beside the different models.

Study and comparison of the "standard" models and optional extras offered provided some interesting information. Some extras although initially expensive merited the added cost by giving longer engine life and requiring less maintenance. Optional engines, with or without liquid propane gas conversions (L.P.G.), are of interest. Write or phone the factory sales manager and see which optional extras he recommends after reviewing your particular needs.

A dealer may quote a price for a standard model plaster/mortar mixer which has a small standard displacement, die-cast aluminum block engine. A talk with the factory sales manager reveals that overall reliability and engine life could be prolonged if the optional L.P.G. carburetor conversion kit was installed. However, L.P.G. gives a 15 percent horsepower drop, as compared to gasoline-powered engines; this coupled with overloading of the mixer for any length of time would lead to an early failure of the engine. This could very easily happen when one is mixing mortar and adding steel or iron punchings to make ballast concrete. When using heavyweight aggregates such as Barite, weights of ballast concrete will be somewhere in the 200-lbs. cu.-ft. range, as opposed to the 140-lbs. cu.-ft. range for normal weight concrete mortar. So from the standpoint of premature engine failure overloading can be a problem.

The standard, gasoline fueled, aluminum block engine with the L.P.G. conversion kit installed will not handle overloads. A simple solution suggested by the sales manager was . . . get two options. A cast-iron engine with the L.P.G. conversion kit installed provides an engine that can operate for long periods of time with an overload and also give a dependable, maintenance-free operating life for the engine. Even with the 15 percent power drop, horsepower will equal, or slightly exceed the standard gasoline-powered engine. Thus the engine life will equal three standard gasoline-fueled engines

1

and give complete dependability, even when constantly being overloaded. Unlike gas-oline, liquid propane gas does not dilute the engine oil or form acids and this lack of acids promotes the longer engine operating life. So these two options, used by commer-cial builders and construction companies, give a dependable piece of equipment that will save money over the long run.

Be wary of the bargain or loss-leader pieces of equipment that manufacturers offer these days. In this class are the one-half to one-bag mortar mixers. They will accom-plish small jobs but they will not do when it comes to ferro-cement boat construction. Remember, it takes one person to charge and run the machine, whether it is a small one or a larger size machine. After talking to the sales manager it was decided that the

Fig. 1-1. A plaster/mortar mixer, Model 8-HN, "Hoe-Boy," manufactured by the Construction Machinery Company, Waterloo, Iowa.

Model 6-N mortar mixer would suit my needs. This mixer has a large mixing capacity but if the crew size wasn't up to using the total mixer capacity, smaller batches could be used. With a smaller machine one is limited to the amount of mortar that can be mixed in one load.

While discussing equipment the sales manager mentioned that his company exported mixers to Africa and that most of the mixers had the cast-iron block engines with kerosene-burning conversion kits installed. He explained that in countries where gas-oline was in short supply and expensive, kerosene was inexpensive and always available.

So, for the economy-minded the kerosene-burning conversion kit may be the answer to high fuel cost.

The largest manufacturer of mortar mixers, The Construction Machinery Company, P.O. Box 120, Waterloo, Iowa, 50704, U.S.A., makes mixers in various sizes from 1-cu. ft. up to 8-cu. ft. models. The standard Model 6-N will have an approximate price of $510.00 FOB factory.

Concrete Vibrator

One other major piece of equipment needed is a small electric or gas-powered concrete vibrator. Since hull thickness will only be about an inch a small vibrator is adequate, see Fig. 1-2. The Stow Model 71-E "Baby Brute" is a fine example with an overall weight of 13 lbs. Prices will range from $60.00 to $80.00, so write to the manufacturer for a list of dealers in the United States and abroad. Also request catalog No. 660 (revision A), which has a list of various grinding and finishing tools needed to finish both green and dry concrete. The company address is: The Stow Manufacturing Company, 443 State Street, Binghamton, New York, 13902, U.S.A. (TWX607-772-0234; phone: 607-723-644).

Vibrations of the vibrator must be on the order of no less than 9,000 impulses per minute. A vibrator is essential to insure complete mortar penetration in hard-to-get-to

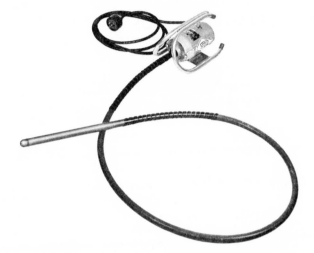

Fig. 1-2. The Stow Model 71-E "Baby Brute" concrete vibrator.

places, i.e., keel, corners, around pipe hull frames, etc. The "cheap" vibrators offered in some magazines are not a wise investment so do not compromise on quality when shopping for a vibrator. Deal with reputable manufacturers or dealers and if in doubt check with local concrete contractors or construction companies.

Basic Tools and Equipment

For the builder renting the major items, i.e., plaster/mortar mixer and cement mortar vibrator some basic items are discussed. Wheelbarrows and enough trowels for members of the plastering team will have to be borrowed, purchased or rented. Be sure to obtain a number of trowels in various sizes including some corner and pie-shaped trowels for those difficult corners and integral tanks. If corner trowels are not available have your local welding shop make some. Mortarboards and hods can be made from scrap lumber. Buckets, shovels and hose are needed to complete the basic tools and equipment required to plaster a ferro-cement hull.

If wheelbarrows are not going to be used consider renting a mortar/plaster pump. Freshly mixed mortar is dumped into the hopper of the mortar/plaster pump and the nozzle operator directs the mortar into those areas to be plastered. This item is a luxury but it will prevent many sore back and arm muscles.

The basic pieces of equipment which can be used with ferro-cement are:

1. Mortar/plaster mixer, 6 to 10 cu. ft. capacity. Approximate cost — $650.00 — $800.00

2. Plaster/mortar pump and hoses, 10 cu. ft. capacity. Approximate cost — $3,500.00.

3. Gunite Rig, including water pump. Approximate cost — $2,800.00 — $3,900.00 (3/4 cu. yd. to 1 1/2 to 2 cu. yd. capacity).

4. Air compressor, engine-driven, 125 CFM and up. Approximate cost — $3,500.00 and up to $12,000.00.

5. Selected spare parts ($1,000.00, estimated).

The basic functions of this equipment are: mixing of mortar and the mixing and placement of mortar.

The equipment in three groups range from simple to complex. As arranged, Groups II and III enable the ferro-cement builder to accomplish two things; faster placement of mortar and the use of lower cost, smaller opening (1/4") plasterer's expanded metal lath.

GROUP I

Plaster/Mortar Mixer or Mixers

This represents the very basic and minimum equipment required for building ferro-cement hulls. A horizontal rotating blade makes a dry homogeneous mass of the aggregates, cement, pozzolan and water. To promote longer engine life with a minimum of unscheduled maintenance the mortar mixer should be equipped with the larger cast-iron engine and the L.P.G. burning conversion kit.

Using mortar mixers without a mortar/plaster pump limits the builder to the use of 1/2 inch or larger opening poultry netting. The cost of this type mesh is high, approximately .04 1/2 cents per square foot, wholesale, FOB San Francisco. Expanded metal lath costs $20.00 for 600 sq. ft. compared to $27.00 per roll of wire mesh (4 x 150 ft. roll, 600 sq. ft.). Hand placement of mortar through several layers of 3/8 or 1/4 inch openings is extremely difficult, if not impossible.

GROUP II

Plaster/Mortar Mixer, 6-10 cu. ft. capacity; Plaster/Mortar Pump, 10 cu. ft. capacity

This group has the addition of a plaster/mortar pump, which is used to force mortar into and through the hull membrane under pressure. The mortar is mixed as usual, dumped directly into the plaster/mortar pump hopper (see Fig. 1-3), and pumped under pressure through rubber hose into the hull. The equipment is reliable if maintained on a schedule. L.P.G. conversions are recommended. Placement of mortar is fast with the elimination of wheelbarrow walks and a large platform. The reduction of "hod" carriers allows more workers to get actual finishing experience and/or more workers can place mortar. The use of the less expensive plasterer's expanded lath, several layers of it on both sides of the hull membrane, is another advantage. Smaller openings (3/8-in. and 1/4-in.) dictate that only mortar *under pressure* will *completely* penetrate the membrane.

The skill level of the operator need not be high, nor does the operator have to have a lot of experience. An important consideration with this equipment group is maintaining adequate training for the plaster/mortar pump clean-up and maintenance men.

Trained maintenance personnel who can trouble-shoot are a must. A stock of spare parts and complete assemblies, i.e., plaster/mortar pump and engine for quick replacement will prevent long periods of wasted time. One company manufacturing plaster/mortar pumps is the Essick Mfg. Co., 850 Woodruff Lane, Elizabeth, New Jersey, U.S.A.

GENERAL SPECIFICATIONS

ENGINE:	18 H.P. 2 Cylinder Wisconsin Air Cooled Model T.H.D.
PUMP:	Essick 3 Piston Machine — Direct Drive with Torque Limiter
AIR COMPRESSOR	Duplex 10 Cubic Foot Per Minute Quincy Model 210
HOPPER:	10 Cubic Foot Capacity — Corten Steel.
NET WEIGHT:	1703 Lbs.
MATERIAL HOSE:	High Pressure Dacron Reinforced Plaster Hose — Optional Equipment.

Fig. 1-3. Essick P-18 plaster/mortar pump.

GROUP III

Mortar Mixer; (Hopper, Nozzle, Hose, Water Pump); Gunite Rig; Air Compressor, Gas-Driven

This group of equipment is the most expensive and certainly the most complicated to maintain. The gunite rig will accomplish two things that the other two groups are not able to accomplish: elimination of retardants and air-entrainment agents, and placement of extremely dry mortar into and through the mesh. Gunite-placed mortar will have significantly stronger compressive strengths.

Again, plasterer's expanded lath or other fine mesh may be used. Another big advantage is that of extremely quick placement of mortar with a minimum of finishing.

Disadvantages to this group are serious. The nozzle operator, like the plaster finisher, will find it is an individual craft, learned only from long experience. Bounce-back of mix and separation of aggregates and cement is a constant problem so careful attention while applying mortar is a must. Another problem, sand voids in random sections of the hull are very hard to detect.

Maintenance of equipment can be a problem, especially if one has to train personnel while operating equipment. Spare parts are also a problem because most items are hard to get and are usually proprietary or in-house-manufactured. The final disadvantage is cost. This equipment is expensive.

Recommendations: I highly recommend Group II be considered the best choice. The equipment (plaster/mortar pump) is small, of modest cost, and can place mortar as fast as the gunite rig without the operator training and skills that are required on gunite.

Another advantage is that we can place mortar *through* the membrane housing and the mortar will not have occasional sand spots. Also, strength will be as figured because the mortar will be precisely mixed with a known water content, as opposed to variables caused by the nozzle operator.

A review of the different group costs shows that for $3,000 more the builder can step up from Group I to Group II and save money on materials cost and mortar placement time if he is producing a series of hulls.

Group III, with an additional cost of $3,500 over Group II, gives one main advantage — that of placing an almost dry mortar. The degree of dryness of the mortar has many variables and the nozzle operator's skill is of the utmost importance. If the compressor or some other component of the gunite rig fails, then the builder must resort to hand placement of mortar. This will be next to impossible if metal lath is used on the hull.

If Group II is purchased, allocate $900 to $1,000 for spare parts and built-up assemblies for on-the-spot repairs. This group is the best buy because relatively unskilled workers can be trained in mixing, pumping, and placing mortar, and in good maintenance practices. Also large savings on materials can accrue over a long-term period with Group II.

The cost comparison chart compares the three groups.

Cost Comparison Chart

	Group I			Group II			Group III	
Qty.	Equipment	Cost	Qty.	Equipment	Cost	Qty.	Equipment	Cost
2 ea.	Mixer	$1,200	1 ea.	Mixer	$ 600	1 ea.	Mixer	$ 600
			1 ea.	Plaster/ Cement Pump	$3,500	1 ea.	Gunite Rig	$3,500
						1 ea.	Compressor, 125 CFM	$3,500
	TOTAL:	$1,200		TOTAL:	$4,100		TOTAL:	$7,600

II

MATERIALS

Cement

A basic understanding of concrete and the components that make up a high quality concrete is necessary to produce a first-rate ferro-cement hull. Use the finest quality ingredients available, plus the correct mixing and application methods, to obtain the best quality concrete for your hull.

About 10 to 15 percent of the total volume of concrete consists of hydraulic cement. Cement is used in the smallest quantity of all the ingredients in concrete and is the most expensive. When water is mixed with the cement a paste is formed, this paste is the cementing medium which binds the aggregates together into a solid state. The correct amount of water, when mixed with the cement, determines the quality of the paste. Figure 2-1 shows the strengths obtainable using various amounts of water in relation to bags of cement. This is called the Water/Cement ratio (W/C) and is always expressed in pounds or gallons of water to a bag of cement.

Water Cement Ratio Gals. of Water Per Bag of Cement (U. S. 94-lbs.)	Compressive Strength (At 28 days-PSI)
9-gal./bag	2,000-psi
8 "	2,500 "
7 "	3,200 "
6 "	4,000 "
5 "	5,000 "
4 "	6,000 "

Fig. 2-1. Effect of water content on compressive strength of concrete (non-air-entrained concrete).

Although there are many types of cement, only those pertinent to ferro-cement are listed:

ASTM Type I Cement

This is the general all-purpose cement used where cement is not subjected to high sulfate action from soils, sea water, or to an objectionable heat rise from hydration. Uses include sidewalks, reinforced concrete buildings, water towers, reservoirs, concrete pipe, masonry blocks, ferro-cement hulls, and floating docks.

ASTM Type II Cement

Type II cement was developed for moderate resistance to sulphate attack, such as in drainage structures where the ground waters are fairly high in sulphate. Also included here would be sea water. Type II is used for mass structures, such as heavy sea retaining walls, piers, and abutments. It is used because of its ability to minimize temperature rise, especially when placed in hot weather. This is an excellent, moderate-cost cement to use for ferro-cement hulls and other structures, such as floating docks, and holding tanks for sewage and fuels.

7

ASTM Type III, High Early-Strength Cement

This cement was developed so that it would cure much faster than either type I or type II, and for the early removal of forms where quicker use of the concrete is desired. Its shorter curing period allows use in cold weather, and it is a favorite with the building industry.

ASTM Type V, Sulphate-Resisting Cement

This cement is used where there is extremely high sulphate action, such as in ground waters and soils high in sulphate content. Uses include sewage pipe where there are sewage gasses present. Exposed and non-painted hull surfaces constantly exposed to sea water should be of type V sulfate resistant cement. The cost of type V cement is considerably higher than type I cement, but for a longlasting hull it is the number one choice and a must where non-painted, floating diesel fuel and sewage tanks are to be built.

The British equivalents to the ASTM types of cement follow:

Type I: Ordinary Portland Cement, to British Standard Specification 12.
Type II: No direct equivalent but the following cements can comply:
           Low-Heat Portland Cement to B.S. 1370.
           Portland Blast-Furnace Cement to B.S. 146.*
           Sulphate-Resisting Portland Cement to B.S. 4027.
Type III: Rapid-Hardening Portland Cement to B.S. 12.
Type V: Sulphate-Resisting Portland Cement to B.S. 4027.

White Portland Cement

This is the most expensive and a luxury item. The principal difference from normal grey cement is its white color. The whiteness is obtained by using materials which contain a minimum amount of iron and manganese oxide.

The specific gravity of Portland cement is 3.15 and this figure is used in calculating the various mix proportions. It is not an indication of strength.

Specific costs for the different types of cement vary from one region to another. A big expense is transportation. Types II or V may have to be specially ordered if they are not widely used in a region. This is generally the case if high sulphate conditions are not present in the soil of a particular region.

Types I, II and III are normally available, with type I cement being the least expensive of the four types, about $1.50 to $1.70 per bag of cement. Types II and III will be slightly higher in cost, usually about 10 to 15 cents more per bag. Type V will be slightly higher than types II and III, since type V is certified to be highly sulphate-resistant, and it requires more steps in the manufacturing process than the others. Local cement companies will quote exact prices on the various types of cement.

Aggregates

Aggregates, the least expensive ingredients used in concrete, comprise 66 to 78 percent of the total volume. Particle shape, graduation, and maximum size are impor-

---

*It should be noted that mainly ordinary Portland and sulphate-resisting Portland cements, and perhaps Portland blast-furnace cement, would be used in parts of Scotland.

tant factors in a quest for strong, dense concrete. Two classifications define aggregate sizes:

Fine aggregates consist of natural sand, manufactured sand, or a combination of both graded in size from 1/4 in. maximum size to near dust size.

Coarse aggregates — washed and graded crushed stone, gravel, or blast-furnace slag — are not used in ferro-cement mortar since the particle size ranges from 1/4 in. and over.

The proper grading of fine aggregates is of the utmost importance, for it insures dense stacking, or near solid arrangement of particles in the concrete. Fine aggregates must be suitably graded from coarse to fine. This grading serves three vital purposes: contributes to the workability and uniformity of the concrete; insures that the concrete is as dense as possible, making for maximum watertightness; obtains good finishability on the concrete by having sufficient well-graded fine aggregates and cement particles in the mix.

The shape of the particles has special significance. Very sharp or rough particles, or flat elongated pieces, require more fine materials (fine sand or pozzolan, which is natural or artificial volcanic ash) to produce workable concrete than do aggregates rounded or cubical in shape.

Aggregate producers state that a fineness modulus range of 2.40 to 2.80 will produce an excellent dense concrete with good finishability characteristics. Fineness modulus is a term used as an index to denote the fineness or coarseness of aggregates. This graduation is accomplished by passing sand through a series of sieves of increasing fineness. These sieves are sized according to the number of openings per square inch. Thus a No. 4 sieve would have four openings per square inch, a No. 30 sieve would have 30 openings per square inch, and so on. The cumulative percentages of sand retained on each of the series of finer and finer sieves are added and then divided by 100, which gives fineness modulus (F.M.). See Fig. 2-2.

Sieve Size	Percent of Sand Retained (Cumulative)
No. 4	2.0
No. 8	20.0
No. 16	30.0
No. 30	60.0
No. 50	74.0
No. 100	90.0
F. M.	276.0 ÷ 100 = 2.76

Fig. 2-2. Computation of fineness modulus.

The amounts of sand passing through the No. 50 sieve and No. 100 sieve affects the denseness, workability, and finishability. Ferro-cement mix calls for the fine aggregates to contain not less than 30 percent passing the No. 50 sieve and at least five percent passing the No. 100 sieve.

Builders using lightweight aggregates (expanded shale and/or clay), should try to have 35 to 75 percent lightweight aggregate retained on the No. 30 sieve (25 to 65 percent passing). One example of packaged lightweight aggregate is offered by the Basalt Rock Company, Inc., Napa, California, 94559, U.S.A. Its specifications are shown in Fig. 2-3.

Interest is quite high in ferro-cement in Australia, and the Cement and Concrete Association of Australia provides free and impartial information on the many uses of cement and aggregates for use in ferro-cement. They have done and are continuing to do research on ferro-cement. The Association has two gradings for sand used in ferro-cement. Grade #1 is for the normal thickness of hull, where the mesh openings are 1/2-in. or larger, and Grade #2 is for a thinner hull where the mesh or plasterer's lath has openings of 1/2-in. *or less*. The grading curves are shown in Fig. 2-4. It is also advised that due to the higher percentage of fines in Grading #2, a higher cement content should be used, and should not fall below 60 lbs. of cement per cubic foot of sand.

Sand (#4 × 0)

Specific Gravity	- 2. 05
Unit Weight (loose moist)	- 60 to 68
Absorption	- 10%
Sand Equivalent (S. E.)	- 95 to 100
Fineness Modulus (F. M.)	- 2. 7 to 3. 1

Sieve Size	Percent of Sand Passing
No. 4	99. 0
No. 8	82. 0
No. 16	56. 0
No. 30	36. 0
No. 50	23. 0
No. 100	12. 0

Fig. 2-3. Specifications of a packaged lightweight aggregate.

Grading #1

B.S. Sieve Size or No.	3/16	7	14	25	52	100	200
% Passing By Weight	100	100	85	55	15	4	3

B. S. -British Sieve.

Grading #2

B.S. Sieve Size or No.	3/16	7	14	25	52	100	200
% Passing By Weight	100	100	100	98	30	2	1

Fig. 2-4. Sand grading curves of the Cement and Concrete Assn. of Australia.

Chapter XII explains that lightweight aggregates were used in the first large reinforced concrete ships and some of this concrete is still in good condition after 30 years of exposure to sea water, tidal action and weathering action of the atmosphere. Strengths obtained then can be obtained today. The use of the expanded shale and clays in lieu of normal weight sand aggregates will give something on the order of a 20 percent weight reduction, which can thus be utilized elsewhere in extra fuel, or what have you.

Other extra lightweight aggregates, such as perlite and vermiculite are known as insulating lightweight aggregates and will produce concrete having only a compressive strength of about 1,000 psi (pounds per square inch). These two types should not be used for structural concrete, and therefore are not suitable for ferro-cement because of this low strength. As of this writing, the author has not heard of anyone who has used these aggregates for ferro-cement. Perlite and vermiculite are used in the construction industry for lightweight roofing and insulating concrete.

Additional information can be obtained by writing to members of the Expanded Shale and Clay Institute:

The Expanded Shale and Clay Institute
National Press Building
Washington, D.C.

Domtar Construction Materials, Ltd.
P.O. Box 216, Station "F"
Toronto, Canada

British Colombia Lightweight Aggregates, Ltd.
813-475 Howe Street
Vancouver, B.C., Canada

A.G. Hunziker & Cie
Lagerstrasse 1
Zurich, Switzerland

Lite-Crete Aggregates, Div. of CECEC
Developments Pty., Ltd.
P. O. Box 58, Homebush
New South Wales, Australia

Albion Reid Pty., Ltd.
141 A Arden Street, North Melbourne
Victoria, Australia

Mitsui Mining & Smelting Co., Ltd.
2-Chrome, Nihonbashi-Muromachi
Chuo-Ku, Tokyo, Japan

Admixtures

Modern Portland cement dates from 1756, when John Smeaton, who had been employed by the English government to build a lighthouse in the English Channel, discovered that an impure or clayey limestone, when burned and slaked, would harden into a solid mass under water, as well as in air. The Romans invented and extensively used a lime-volcanic ash (pozzolans) mixture that was superior to the even more ancient lime mortar. The Romans are said to have used blood as an admixture in the lime-volcanic ash mortar. The blood possibly entrained air which would help to improve durability and aid workability.

Admixtures are half again as old as Portland cement. They have been developed to accomplish three things:

1. Reduce the amount of water used in the cement, thus giving a higher strength concrete.

2. Allow more time for placement of concrete in hot weather, retarding the initial set of the mortar.

3. Impart minute air bubbles within the concrete, thus imparting cold weather resistance and giving the concrete a longer life when exposed to alternate freezing and thawing cycles.

Other admixtures include the pozzolans or extra fines which help to make the concrete more dense and thus more watertight. Pozzolans are the primary admixtures used today. They consist of various materials: volcanic materials, fly ash, furnace slag and diatomaceous earth.

The most common pozzolans used today are fly ash and fine diatomaceous earth. These materials vary from region to region, but they will accomplish the job that was intended for them. The addition of these extra fines does not increase the curing time, and the concrete will continue to gain strength over an extended period of time, usually 50 years or so.

If the other types of pozzolans are unavailable, or transportation costs are excessive, another material can be used — finely ground diatomaceous earth. One trade name for diatomaceous earth is "Celatom," another is "Celite." It is packaged in 50-lb. bags. A 1.5 percent mixture by weight of cement to diatomaceous earth will accomplish the same thing as 15 percent by weight of conventional pozzolan materials.

The companies listed as handling the expanded shale and clay aggregates sometimes deal in the pozzolans, so write to them for availability and prices of pozzolan materials. "Celatom" is sold by Eagle-Picher Industries, Inc., American Building, Cincinnati, Ohio, 45201, USA. "Celite" is marketed by the Celite Division, Johns-Manville, 22

East 40th St., New York, N. Y., USA. Builders living overseas should write to either of these companies to order diatomaceous earth.

Air-entrainment, water-retardant agents are handled by numerous concerns and careful research has turned up one company that has dealers world wide, is reputable, and offers quality products and service. The company Master Builders, offers these commercial admixtures: Pozzolith 8, Pozzolith 8A and MB-VR, single-strength, Vinsol Resin. Pozzolith 8 is a water-reducing agent which reduces the needed water content by about 12 percent and, at the same time, gives an initial benefit of 30 to 45 minutes retardation of the mortar. This helps to eliminate cold joints when the builder cannot keep his mortar mixing and placing up with the rate of the setting of previously applied mortar. This retardation is particularly helpful when placing mortar in extremely hot weather. This admixture comes in a powder form and is quite easy to use if weighed, pre-bagged, and added at mixing time.

Pozzolith 8A also is a water-reducing agent which reduces the needed water by 12 percent, gives 30 to 45 minutes retardation of the mortar and has an air-entrainment agent added which imparts three percent to five percent entrained air content to the mortar. This admixture is also available in a powder form and when used should be carefully weighed and bagged prior to actual mortar mixing. Mixing charts for using these admixtures are presented in Chapter V.

MB-VR (Master Builders' Vinsol Resin) single-strength vinsol resin is only an air-entrainment which puts tiny air bubbles into the freshly mixed mortar thus imparting a high resistance to damage from alternate freezing and thawing cycles. This resin comes in liquid form and is of single strength so when ordering be sure that single strength is understood because that is actually what you receive.

Note: Extreme accuracy in dosage of an air-entrainment agent is a must since over-dosage will ruin the structural strength of the concrete. Extra air-entrainment agents will be necessary when working in extremely high temperatures. Check with manufacturer for exact higher dosages and temperature range.

Measure the agent in graduated cylinders prior to mixing mortar. Small drug bottles with screw caps should be used to store the measured doses of resins or powders. Since all air-entrainment agents are not of equal strength use only one brand throughout the mixing of the mortar. The addresses of Master Builders Company offices are:

Master Builders Co.
2490 Lee Boulevard
Cleveland, Ohio 44118

Master Builders Co.
1991 Dennison Street
Oakland, California, 94606

Master Builders Co.
374 Berkshire
London, Ontario

Master Builders Co.
715 W. 7th Avenue
Vancouver 9, B.C.

Tecnocreto S.A. de C.V.
Blvd. M. Avila Camacho #14
Latin American Div. (Antes 1002)
Mexico City 10, D.F., Mexico

Master Builders (Europe) S.A.
12 Dingwall Avenue
Croydon, Surrey CRO2AA, England

Master Builders (Europe) S.A.
3 rue Joseph II
Brussels 4, Belgium

Embecon Pty., Ltd.
25 Anderson Street
Chatswood, N.S.W. 2067
Australia

Nisso Master Builders Co., Ltd.
Empire Bldg. 10-33
Akasaka 4-Chrome, Minato-ku
Tokyo, Japan

Steel

Steel in the form of pipe, rods, and wire mesh will be used in ferro-cement. Naturally, some types are better to use than others.

Black iron pipe is easily worked and welded and suitable to use for the pipe frame method. Figures 2-5 and 2-6 list the two types of pipe, standard and extra strong black iron pipe. The principal difference between the two is wall-thickness. The extra strong pipe will have a smaller inside diameter than the standard pipe and will weigh as much as the next larger size of standard pipe. So, for those wanting to use a smaller pipe size, the answer is to use the extra strong pipe.

Pipe Size	Wall Thickness	Weight Per Ft.	Diameter External	Internal	Weight Per 21-Ft. Length	No. of Lengths Per Bundle	Weight Per Bundle
1/8	0.095	.31	.405	.215	6.51	30	195.0 lbs.
1/4	.119	.54	.540	.320	11.34	24	272.0 "
3/8	.126	.74	.675	.423	15.54	18	280.0 "
1/2	.147	1.09	.840	.546	22.89	12	275.0 "
3/4	.154	1.47	1.050	.724	30.87	7	216.0 "
1	.179	2.70	1.315	.957	45.57	5	228.0 "
1-1/4	.191	3.00	1.660	1.278	63.00	3	189.0 "
1-1/2	.200	3.63	1.900	1.500	76.23	3	229.0 "
2	.218	5.02	2.375	1.939	105.42	1	105.0 "
2-1/2	.276	7.66	2.875	2.323	160.86	1	161.0 "
3	.300	10.25	3.500	2.900	215.25	1	215.0 "
3-1/2	.318	12.51	4.000	3.364	262.71	1	263.0 "

Fig. 2-5. ASTM-A-120: Extra strong pipe — black and galvanized; ASTM-A-53: Coupled and plain ends.

Pipe Size	Wall Thickness	Weight Per Ft.	Diameter External	Internal	Weight Per 21-Ft. Length	No. of Lengths Per Bundle	Weight Per Bundle
1/8	0.068	.24	.405	.269	5.04	30	151.0 lbs.
1/4	.088	.42	.590	.364	8.82	24	212.0 "
3/8	.091	.57	.675	.493	11.97	18	215.0 "
1/2	.109	.85	.840	.622	17.85	12	214.0 "
3/4	.113	1.13	1.050	.824	23.73	7	166.0 "
1	.133	1.68	1.315	1.049	35.28	5	176.0 "
1-1/4	.140	2.28	1.660	1.380	47.88	3	144.0 "
1-1/2	.145	2.93	1.900	1.610	57.33	3	172.0 "
2	.154	3.68	2.375	2.067	77.28	1	77.0 "
2-1/2	.203	5.82	2.875	2.469	122.22	1	122.0 "
3	.216	7.58	3.500	3.068	159.18	1	159.0 "
3-1/2	.226	9.11	4.000	3.548	191.31	1	191.0 "

Fig. 2-6. ASTM-A-120: Standard pipe — black and galvanized; ASTM-A-53: Coupled and plain ends.

Size of Pipe (Inches)	Number of Equivalent Pipes								
	3/8	1/2	3/4	1	1-1/4	1-1/2	2	2-1/2	3
3/8	1								
1/2	1.8	1							
3/4	3.6	2	1						
1	6.6	3.7	1.8	1					
1-1/4	13	7	3.6	2	1				
1-1/2	19	11	5.3	2.9	1.5	1			
2	36	20	10	5.5	2.7	1.9	1		
2-1/2	56	31	16	8	4.3	2.9	2	1	
3	97	54	27	15	7	5	2.8	1.8	1

Note: To find number of smaller pipes equal to a larger size, read down from smaller pipe size, across from larger size; read answer at intersection. Thus, capacity of one 2-1/2 inch pipe equals capacity of eight 1-inch pipes.

Fig. 2-7 Comparative discharge capacity of water piping.

Mfr's Std. Gauge No.	Weight Per Sq. Ft.	Inch Equiv. Steel Sheet
3	10.0000-lbs.	0.2391
4	9.3750 "	0.2242
5	8.7500 "	0.2092
6	8.1250 "	0.1943
7	7.5000 "	0.1793
8	6.8750 "	0.1644
9	6.250 "	0.1495
10	5.6250 "	0.1345
11	5.0000 "	0.1196
12	4.3750 "	0.1046
13	3.7500 "	0.0897
14	3.1250 "	0.0747
15	2.8125 "	0.0673

Fig. 2-8. Standard gauge steel sheets
Weights and Thickness Table.

Bar No.	Weight Lbs./ft.	Dia.	Area	Perimeter	Length Per Bar
2	0.167	0.250	0.05	0.786	20-Feet
3	0.376	0.375	0.11	1.178	20-Feet
4	0.668	0.500	0.20	1.178	20-Feet

Fig. 2-9. Reinforcing bar weights (smooth) and dimensions.

Various types of rods are available and the price depends on the type of rod used. Mild steel rod is a low carbon, "hot rolled" rod suitable for general use in production and maintenance work because it is easily welded and formed. This mild steel rod doesn't have much spring and bends easily. Since these rods tend to sag when strung between two hull frames and subjected to excessive pressure they should not be used in ferro-cement hulls, if at all possible.

A mild steel reinforcing rod used extensively in the construction industry in reinforced concrete is another type available. These rods are suitable to use only where welding is not required because they become quite brittle after welding.

For the spacer rod applications on ferro-cement hulls a high tensile steel rod made from hot rolled steel bars and known as special bar quality stock is recommended. This type rod is used for forging, heat treating and complicated machine operations.

ROUNDS—HOT ROLLED

Merchant Bar Quality - M 1020
3" and larger - Special Bar Quality - C 1018

Low carbon, hot rolled "mild steel" is suitable for general usage in production and maintenance work, due to its excellent welding and forming characteristics.

Special Bar Quality steels are recommended for forging, heat treating and complicated machining operations.

C 1018 C .15/.20 Mn .60/.90 P .04 Max. S .05 Max.
M 1020 C .17/.24 Mn .25/.60 P .04 Max. S .05 Max.

Diameter	Pounds Per Ft.	Stock Lengths	Diameter	Pounds Per Ft.	Stock Lengths
**3/16	.094	20'	3-1/8	26.08	16,20'
**1/4	.167	20'	3-1/4	28.21	20'
**5/16	.261	20'	3-3/8	30.42	16,20'
3/8	.376	20, 40'*	3-1/2	32.71	20'
7/16	.511	20'	3-5/8	35.09	20'
1/2	.668	20, 40'*	3-3/4	37.55	16,20'
9/16	.845	20'	3-7/8	40.10	20'
5/8	1.04	20, 40'*	4	42.73	16,20'
11/16	1.26	16, 20'	4-1/8	45.44	16,20'
3/4	1.50	30, 40'*	4-1/4	48.23	16,20'
13/16	1.76	16, 20'	4-3/8	51.11	16,20'
7/8	2.04	20, 40'*	4-1/2	54.08	16,20'
15/16	2.35	16, 20'	4-5/8	57.12	16,20'
1	2.67	20, 40'*	4-3/4	60.25	16,20'
1-1/16	3.01	16, 20'	5	66.76	16,20'
1-1/8	3.38	20, 40'*	5-1/4	73.60	16,20'
1-3/16	3.77	CHGO	5-1/2	80.78	16,20'
1-1/4	4.17	20, 40*	5-3/4	88.29	16,20'
1-5/16	4.60	16, 20'	6	96.13	16,20'
1-3/8	5.05	20, 40'*	6-1/8	100.18	CHGO
1-7/16	5.52	CHGO	6-1/4	104.31	16,20'
1-1/2	6.01	20, 40'*	6-1/2	112.82	16,20'
1-5/8	7.05	20, 40'*	6-3/4	121.67	16,20'
1-3/4	8.18	20, 40'*	7	130.85	16,20'
1-7/8	9.39	16, 20, 40'*	7-1/4	140.36	16,20'
2	10.68	20, 40'*	7-1/2	150.21	16,20'
2-1/8	12.06	16, 20, 40'*	7-3/4	160.39	16,20'
2-1/4	13.52	20, 40'*	8	170.90	16,20'
2-3/8	15.06	16, 20, 40'*	8-1/4	181.75	16,20'
2-1/2	16.69	20, 40'*	8-1/2	192.93	16,20'
2-5/8	18.40	16, 20, 40'*	8-3/4	204.45	16,20'
2-3/4	20.19	20, 40'*	9	216.30	16,20'
2-7/8	22.07	40'*	9-1/2	241.00	16,20'
3	24.03	20, 40'*	10	267.04	

** Check with your local supplier.

Figure 2-10.

Chicken wire or mesh is the next item to discuss. See Figs. 2-11 & 2-12. There is a lot of chicken wire on the market that is made from cold drawn wire, woven and then galvinized before or after weaving. Wire gauge sizes are normally in the 18-to-22 gauge range, with 18-gauge being the heaviest. This heaviest gauge is highly recommended for ferro-cement. Most chicken or poultry wire is woven with one-inch holes or openings. This is ideal, because with several layers on the hull, the mortar is still rather easy to force through to the other side of the hull membrane, insuring that there will be no voids in the hull. See Fig. 6-7. Wire with smaller openings is hard to get in this country. Steel supply houses contacted were unable to supply the 22-gauge mesh with one-half inch openings that is manufactured by some Belgian and Japanese steel companies.

Weight Per 150-ft. roll			
Inch height	1-inch 18-gauge	Weight per square ft.	No. of layers needed to weigh 2 to 3 lbs. /ft. sq.
18	45.0	.200	10 Layers-2.0-lbs./sq. ft.
24	59.4	.198	11 Layers-2.178-" " "
36	88.0	.195	11 Layers-2.145 " " "
48	117.0	.195	11 Layers-2.145 " " "
60	145.8	.194	11 Layers-2.145 " " "
72	174.6	.194	11 Layers-2.145 " " "

Fig. 2-11. Heavy duty poultry netting (galvanized before weaving).

Weight Per 150-ft. roll			
Inch height	1-inch 18-gauge	Weight per square ft.	No. of layers needed to weigh 2 to 3 lbs. /ft. sq.
18	53.5	.238	10 Layers-2.380-lbs./sq. ft.
24	73.5	.245	11 Layers-2.695 " " "
36	103.1	.229	11 Layers-2.519 " " "
48	136.9	.228	11 Layers-2.508 " " "
60	168.4	.224	11 Layers-2.464 " " "
72	215.0	.238	11 Layers-2.618 " " "

Fig. 2-12. Heavy duty poultry netting (galvanized after weaving).

Metal plasterer's lath is a sheet of thin gauge steel that is run through a series of rollers, cut by circular knives and then pulled apart by a machine. This produces a mesh that is 30 in. x 96 in. and two sizes of diamond-shaped openings are available; one-quarter and three-eighths of an inch. Mesh with the larger openings is preferred since placement of mortar through the finer mesh is extremely difficult unless the mortar is pumped onto the hull under pressure. Plasterer's lath is the least expensive but the most difficult to place mortar through if the builder does not use a plaster/ mortar pump.

The bars, pipes and mesh described are only a few of those available. A talk with local steel supply houses could result in obtaining steel with more desirable working qualities and perhaps at a reduced price.

Water

Water, an important ingredient, will determine the ultimate strength of the concrete. There is a definite relationship between the amount of water used and the quality of the resulting concrete. Increasing the water thins or dilutes the paste, thus reducing the cementing action of the paste. Water does two things: it converts dry cement and aggregates into a plastic workable mass, and reacts with the cement chemically to hydrate and harden the plastic mass into a solid, strong mass.

As shown in the water/cement ratio table Fig. 2-1, this relationship is most important when determining just how strong we want the concrete. To insure a first-quality hull it is essential that the water used in mixing concrete be measured for the first batch and every succeeding batch.

The water used in concrete must be free of acids, alkalies, and oils. Particularly avoid water containing decayed vegetable matter or other organic matter. Drinking water is considered suitable for use in concrete.

III

ADHESIVES

There are several concrete adhesives on the market. One company offers a group of adhesives especially developed for cement that are reasonable in cost. The data available spells out the compressive strength, compressive shear, flexural, and tensile strengths. The Adhesive Engineering Co. offers four structural adhesives and coatings with a relatively long pot, or working life. These four adhesives are listed in Fig. 3-1, and a brief summary lists the particular properties and features of each.

Concresive 1 LPL (Liquid Adhesive)

Concresive 1 LPL has a pot life of about two hours at 75°F. It cures for handling in 48 hours, is ready for full normal service in about five days. Liquid concresive bonds to damp concrete, bonds new concrete to old, bonds old concrete to old, places strongly bonded deck toppings, and patches spalls, deep impressions and deep cracks. A one-inch bolt embedded in Concresive 1 LPL has a pull-out strength of up to 46,000 lbs. Various strengths are:

Bond of new concrete to old . . . .   600 psi with 100% concrete failure
Compressive shear . . . . .1,045 psi
Flexural . . . . 6,000 psi
Compressive yield .11,450 psi
Tensile . . . . 2,720 psi

Concresive 1180 (Paste Adhesive)

Concresive 1180 has a pot life of about 40 minutes at 75°F, cures for use at room temperature in eight hours, and cures in 24 hours at 40°F. This high-strength, low-temperature curing, no-sag, epoxy paste bonds almost all construction materials to concrete and to each other. It is flexible enough to take concrete expansion and contraction, resists acids, water, gasoline and oils, can be applied to dry or wet materials, and has excellent adhesion to steel, aluminum, glass and wood. Typical jobs include bonding neoprene bearing pads to concrete and steel, attaching wood floor plates and sills to concrete slabs and walls, securing polyvinyl chloride and rubber water-stops to concrete, patching shallow voids and spalls in vertical, horizontal and overhead concrete, grouting reinforcing bars, and repairing and resetting broken concrete. Typical strengths with full cure:

Adhesion to concrete . . . . 570 psi with 100% concrete failure
Tensile lap shear on aluminum . . . . .2,400 psi
Tensile lap shear on steel . . . . .2,000 psi

Concresive 1064 (Binder)

Concresive 1064 has a pot life of about 20 minutes at 77°F, cures for service and traffic in about 24 hours and is a low cost binder to use for patching and grouting. Sand aggregates mixed with this binder makes mortar for grouting, or broadcasting on a deck surface for skid resistance. This binder gives long-term resistance to de-icing chemicals, water, sunlight, weathering, oil, grease and gasoline. Other jobs include sealing ferro-cement hulls, filling and leveling hull depressions. Typical properties of the cured adhesive are:

Tensile strength . . . . 800 psi minimum
Tensile elongation 40%

CONCRESIVE	1-LPL	1064	1180	1170
New Concrete to Old	×	0	0	+
Old Concrete to Old	+	+	×	+
Metals to Concrete	+	+	×	+
Bolt Grouting	+	+	×	+
Spall Repairs	+	×	+	+
Non-Skid Membrane Surface	+	×	+	+
Weather Protection	0	+	0	×
Chemical Protection	0	0	0	×
Rumble Strips	0	×	0	0
Interlaminar Membrane Seal	0	×	0	0
Water Stop to Concrete	0	0	×	0
BONDING				
Metals	+	+	×	+
Plastic	0	0	×	0
Rubber	0	0	×	0
Ceramics	+	+	×	+
Cured Concrete	+	+	×	+
Masonry	+	+	×	+
Wood	+	+	×	+

×: Best product for this application
+: Product will also work for this application under some circumstances
0: Product not generally useful for this application

Fig. 3-1. Job applications for concresive structural compounds.

Concresive 1170 (Coating)

Concresive 1170 has a pot life of about 40 minutes at 75°F, and cures fully in seven days at 77°F. This multi-purpose coating protects all concrete hulls and steel. It is tougher and more permanent than ordinary paints or other coatings. An excellent rust inhibitor and barrier to corrosion from sea water and chemicals, it can be sprayed, rolled, or brushed on either interior or exterior surfaces. When mixed with fine sand it is a fully-chemical-resistant, easily-troweled surfacing mortar for diesel tanks, sewage holding tanks, and water tanks. The epoxy aggregate mortar has excellent resistance to sulphuric, hydrochloric and phosphoric acids; sodium and ammonium hydroxide; detergents and water, and is used where alkalies, solvents and chemicals are present.

Typical strengths are:

Tensile . . . . 8,600 psi
Flexural . . . . 16,000 psi
Compressive yield . . . . 13,050 psi
Hardness . . . .   80 Shore D (On Shore seleroscope scale)

Special sealing adhesives available for small jobs are listed.

The numbers of the Concresive products that meet special requirements are:

Bond concrete under water, coat concrete and steel in splash zone 1078
Bond new concrete or plaster indoors to concrete, wood, or steel 1069
Fast setting paste adhesive to bond most dry construction materials, and cure down
    to 20° F. 1209
Pourable polysulphide joint sealant-Ad-Seal 5101
Primer and sealer for wet concrete 7008
Corrosion-inhibiting epoxy primer for steel surfaces 7010
Fast, self-releasing form coating for plywood forms 7022
Liquid hand cleaner for epoxy resins 6001

The Concresive products are made by the Adhesive Engineering Company, 1411 Industrial Road, San Carlos, California, 94070, USA. [TWX: (415) 594-9947; Phone: (415) 591-2686.]

IV

HULL CONSTRUCTION

Plant and Facilities Layout

To find a site suitable for ferro-cement construction the builder should investigate various locations. The area acquired must fill these requirements: have an available supply of water and electricity, plus a good drainage system. Any site that does not have access to water, which is needed for launching the hull, must also have: adequate vertical and horizontal door clearance; sufficient floor strength to support the work platform and the weight of the hull. The hull will be transported on a flatbed trailer, so the work area must allow enough space to maneuver the trailer close to the platform.

Various sites and platform types are discussed in the order of preference.

The Floating Platform. The least expensive to build is the floating platform, constructed on empty 55-gallon drums, interconnected with pipe. This platform may then be sunk or raised by pumping water in or out of the drums. Support timbers are secured on the drums and covered with planking or plywood. Side support timbers are erected, siding nailed on, window openings cut, and the structure roofed over. The hull is built on this platform and after curing and finishing operations are completed, the platform is submerged, allowing the hull to float free. Another method to consider is that of placing pipe rollers between the keel and platform. Wedges can be used to secure the rollers. The hull can then be rolled off the platform into the water at launching time. Steel drums (55-gallon) are quite reasonable in cost and will support about 458-lbs. while floating in the water. A platform that will support 24-tons will require about 120 drums, for a 20 x 40 platform. Remember to subtract the weight of the platform and drums when calculating platform capacity. Supporting brackets to secure the drums to the underside of the platform can be fabricated from wood timbers or steel stock, in the form of rods, angle, flat stock, etc. To keep rusting to a minimum, paint barrels and steel supporting brackets with a good polyester paint. The floating platform is the most economical method, considering the cost of transporting a hull over any distance by a drayage firm.

Low Bank Property. A site near or on a low bank property with water of sufficient depth will eliminate the cost for transporting the hull. This saving on transportation can be used on the boat itself. The keel and work platform can be built in the usual manner, and some sort of marine railway should be constructed so that pipe may be used as rollers with which to launch the hull into the water. Large timbers may be used for track, and if a large enough size is not available, two-by-six timbers may be bolted together to achieve the needed size. Use enough two-by-four or two-by-six timbers for railroad-type ties to get everything rigid. See Fig. 4-1.

Since sites on the water are difficult to locate other working areas are discussed and the necessary requirements for the construction sites are explained.

Backyard. The builder's backyard may be satisfactory if the space between buildings allows for the movement of the completed hull. The ground must be firm enough to support the weight of the truck, trailer, and the hull. If the ground or driveway is soft or wet four-by-eight plywood sheets or other boards of sufficient width laid on the ground will spread the tire load over a larger area.

Barns. Old barns usually have good vertical and horizontal door clearance and plenty of exposed beams to support the hull pipe frames. Make certain that there is enough room to move a flatbed trailer up to the work platform.

Warehouses and Industrial Plants. Warehouses and old industrial plants offer good working space, water, electricity and concrete floor with a drainage system. These are the factors a professional builder considers when looking for a building in which to produce ferro-cement hulls on a commercial basis. The requirements and cover needed for a site are dependent on the weather and the region. A cold climate would require a closed building that could be heated and the warmer regions would not need as much cover or protection.

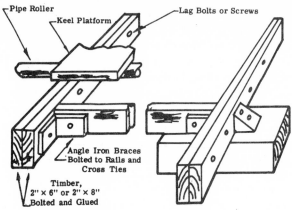

Fig. 4-1. Marine railway construction.

Shed. If a shed is to be erected at the construction site scout lumber companies for bargain materials. Any siding on sale such as, 3/16-in. masonite sheets, 1/8-in. plywood, 1/4-in. plywood, or polyethylene in any width or length can be used on the shed. Some lumber companies offer lots of two-by-fours cut to eight-foot lengths at bargain prices. The timbers can be used by gluing and bolting them together. The side framing timbers could be two-by-fours or two-by-sixes. Using old wooden sash frames and windows will save time, if the windows do not have glass in them a covering of clear plastic will let in light. This natural light is important when it is time for finishing the hull because the gray cement is hard to see in even a well-lighted interior.

The shed must have a supply of running water and good drainage under the work platform is necessary so the mixer can be washed down frequently.

Utilities. 110-V for lights and 220-V for tools and an arc welder are essential. The arc welder will be used extensively welding the keel, bow, stern pipes and horizontal bars. The 220-V current is needed for the arc welder and could be used to hook up a second-hand clothes dryer. The dryer could be used to provide heat in the shed.

Before building a shed or workshop consult the local building inspector and obtain a permit, if one is needed.

Consider the available locations and decide which best fills the requirements: working space, horizontal and vertical door clearance, floor strength, electricity, running water and a good drainage system. Compare the cost of renting space with the cost of building a shed. Use a little imagination when investigating building sites. An area filled with old junk could be suitable and perhaps it could be obtained rent-free for the labor involved in cleaning the space out.

Building Platforms. The fixed building platform can be simple but it must be sturdy. See Figs. 4-2 A,B,C,D. Consult a retired carpenter for advice if you are not familiar with correct procedures for building a platform. When the hull site is some distance from the water the platform should be an inch or two higher than a heavy 40-foot flatbed trailer. This will make it possible to roll the hull right onto the trailer and eliminate the cost of a crane lifting the hull at one location. A truck mounted, 20-ton

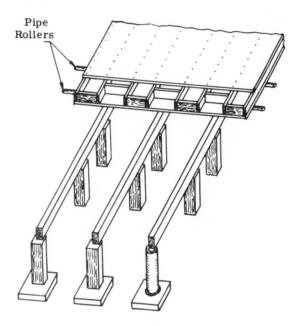

Fig. 4-2A. Platform structure.

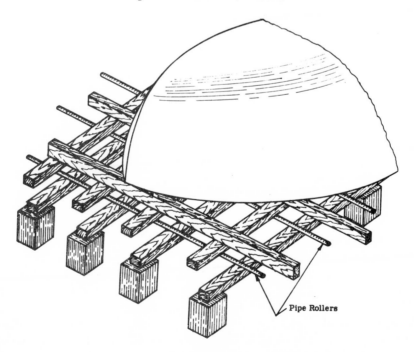

Fig. 4-2B. Platform structure.

cranes cost approximately $65.00 per hour, plus high mileage costs. The hull can be rolled from either the upright or upside down position. To keep the hull in an upright position side support timbers must be used and it is necessary to have a sliding platform that is built on top of pipe rollers that are laid down on the fixed building platform. This sliding platform (Fig. 4-2A) is also needed with the hull in the upside down position, but the hull must then be turned over at the launching site.

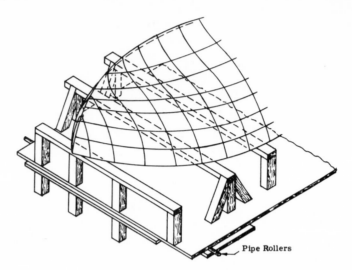

Fig. 4-2C. Platform structure.

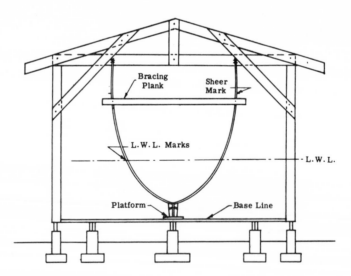

Fig. 4-2D. Pipe mold method shows both setting up pipe frames and some shed construction details.

The platform as seen in Fig. 4-2A shows foundation blocks on three-foot centers and timbers bolted down. It is imperative that this platform be level and that the upright timbers are absolutely vertical, 90 degrees from the level platform. If the pipe roller method is used put roller pipe down and start to build the sliding platform on top of the pipes. The plywood or planks must be securely nailed to the two-by-fours, and the six-inch centers must be maintained under the keel or the edges of the inverted hull.

Three-quarter-inch plywood is excellent for the platform covers. Remember to fasten the top sliding platform securely.

If building from the ground up, clay or sewage pipes may be utilized as forms in which to pour concrete. Figure 4-2A shows the placement of concrete forms. The upright hull requires a sturdy platform which will support the workers applying mortar and finishing the hull. The platform allows easy movement around the hull and a suitable scaffolding system may also be necessary. For the inverted hull, the platform isn't quite as important but it allows the worker to put stands inside the hull to smooth out the interior. The inverted hull sides are placed on raised mounts (see Figs. 4-2B & C), so workers placing mortar can use stands and have easy access to the interior of the hull. The platform around the hull should extend at least four feet beyond the widest part of the hull. This allows for the placement of stands or scaffolds and the workers have sufficient room to work while others are carrying mortar to different parts of the hull.

For the open-pipe frame method (Fig. 4-2D), side supporting timbers must be well secured into the ground and also to the roof supporting timbers, in a warehouse or barn.

Fig. 4-3. The 55-gallon drums used to support the hull are an inexpensive substitute for a more extensive support platform. The completed open mold frame with stringers fastened to the station frames is ready for spacer bars and mesh.

If a support platform seems to be a bit on the expensive side, then consider using 55-gallon drums (see Fig. 4-3). One word of caution here: make certain that the drums are not cocked to one side and are not resting on humps or inclines. Since the hull is upside down you can get to the inside of it and will be able to finish off the inside and to fill any voids left due to inadequate penetration of mortar, which will be applied mostly from the outside.

Lofting Hints

Boat projects of any size require a pattern that will enable the builder to transfer given dimensions to the material so the actual shape can be outlined on the material with suitable instruments. This initial step, drawing the shape of the hull full-scale on a platform or floor from plans is called "laying down."

The next step, drawing of templates, hull shapes or station frames, is called "taking off."

Boat blueprints are shown in three projections:

Profile: Shows side view with actual lengths and heights, with widths foreshortened.

Plan: Shows bottom view with actual lengths and widths, with heights foreshortened.

Body Plan: Shows end views with actual widths and heights, with lengths foreshortened.

The table of offsets must be thoroughly understood. It contains heights from the baseline and widths from the centerline at enough stations so the shape of the hull can be drawn full-size on a lofting floor. These dimensions are given in feet, inches, and eighths. Thus, 3,6,6 means three feet, six, and six-eighths inches.

Remember that: 1/4″ = 2/8″; 1/2″ = 4/8″; 3/4″ = 6/8″. All engineering scales read in feet, inches, and fractions to help eliminate errors. Reduce all dimensions to inches to make dividing easier and avoid arithmetical errors. A chart for the quick conversion of feet to inches is given in Fig. 4-4.

	2 Ft.	3 Ft.	4 Ft.	5 Ft.	6 Ft.
0″	24″	36″	48″	60″	72″
1″	25″	37″	49″	61″	73″
2″	26″	38″	50″	62″	74″
3″	27″	39″	51″	63″	75″
4″	28″	40″	52″	64″	76″
5″	29″	41″	53″	65″	77″
6″	30″	42″	54″	66″	78″
7″	31″	43″	55″	67″	79″
8″	32″	44″	56″	68″	80″
9″	33″	45″	57″	69″	81″
10″	34″	46″	58″	70″	82″
11″	35″	47″	59″	71″	83″

Fig. 4-4. Conversion of feet to inches.

The hull transom is developed as a true plane to get its actual shape, since it isn't shown in its true shape in other views.

A large, smooth lofting platform or floor is desirable to develop the full-size hull length, frames and transom. To make the lines easier to see paint the surface light gray. A plywood platform that can be propped up against any convenient wall when the lofting is finished is satisfactory and propping it against the wall when bending frames will eliminate the need to lean over all the time. Lofting requires study and practice. There are numerous books devoted exclusively to this aspect of boatbuilding.

An excellent book that clearly explains lofting procedures is *Boatbuilding In Your Own Backyard*, by S. S. Rabl, 1958 (Chapter 4, *Laying Down and Taking Off*); Cornell Maritime Press, Cambridge, Maryland.

For a book covering the complete design and lofting aspects, including figuring displacement and sail area, computation of ballast, and preparation of written specifications, see *The Elements of Yacht Design*, by Norman L. Skene (revised by Francis S. Kinney); Dodd, Mead & Co., New York, New York.

The actual laying down of the hull should be preceded by a study of these books. Contact a local boat builder or drafting instructor for help with lofting problems.

Most boats are designed to the outside of the hull planking. This is done so that the thickness of the hull planking will not put an error into the displacement calculations. If this wasn't taken into consideration, the boat would float higher in the water than designed. This is especially true of ferro-cement hulls over 30 feet in length.

When making hull frame templates, *subtract* the thickness of the hull from the already drawn outside hull dimension line. This can be done by drawing in another line inside the previously drawn outside hull line. This inside line will then represent the outer edge of the hull frame.

Inches	0	1	2	3	4	5	6	7	8	9	10	11
0		.0833	.1667	.2500	.333	.4167	.500	.5833	.6667	.750	.8333	.9167
1/16	.0052	.0885	.1719	.2552	.3385	.4219	.5052	.5885	.6719	.7552	.8385	.9219
1/8	.0104	.0937	.1771	.2604	.3437	.4271	.5104	.5937	.6771	.7604	.8437	.9271
3/16	.0156	.0990	.1823	.2656	.3490	.4323	.5156	.5990	.6823	.7656	.8490	.9323
1/4	.0208	.1042	.1875	.2708	.3542	.4375	.5208	.6042	.6875	.7708	.8542	.9375
5/16	.0260	.1094	.1927	.2760	.3594	.4427	.5260	.6094	.6927	.7760	.8594	.9427
3/8	.0312	.1146	.1979	.2812	.3646	.4479	.5339	.6172	.7005	.7839	.8672	.9505
7/16	.0365	.1198	.2031	.2865	.3698	.4531	.5365	.6198	.7031	.7865	.8698	.9531
1/2	.0417	.1250	.2083	.2917	.3750	.4583	.5417	.6250	.7083	.7917	.8750	.9583
9/16	.0469	.1302	.2135	.2969	.3802	.4635	.5469	.6302	.7135	.7969	.8802	.9635
5/8	.0521	.1354	.2188	.3021	.3854	.4688	.5521	.6354	.7188	.8021	.8854	.9688
11/16	.0573	.1406	.2240	.3073	.3906	.4740	.5573	.6406	.7240	.8073	.8906	.9740
3/4	.0625	.1458	.2292	.3125	.3958	.4792	.5625	.6458	.7292	.8125	.8958	.9792
13/16	.0677	.1510	.2344	.3177	.4010	.4844	.5677	.6510	.7344	.8177	.9010	.9844
7/8	.0729	.1562	.2396	.3229	.4062	.4896	.5729	.6562	.7396	.8229	.9062	.9896
15/16	.0781	.1615	.2448	.3281	.4115	.4948	.5781	.6615	.7448	.8281	.9115	.9949

Fractions of an Inch (row label, leftmost column)

Fig. 4-5. Conversion of inches and fractions to decimal parts of a foot.

Most boat designs can safely be changed 25 percent above or below their designed length and still maintain the same overall proportions. All dimensions would have to be enlarged or reduced proportionally as the case may be.

The formula for direct proportion is: A is to B as C is to X, or A:B :: C:X.

For example, where:

A=24 ft. (Length of present boat)

B=30 ft. (Length of proposed boat)

C= 1 ft. (Any individual dimension on present boat)

X=Unknown (Corresponding individual dimension on proposed boat)

The rule is to multiply the means and divide by the extremes.

Thus: 24:30 :: 1:X,

30 times 1 = 30 ft.,

```
        1.25
   24|30.00
      24
      60
      48
     120
     120
```

Fig. 4-6A. The initial layer of mesh and horizontal bars wired into position. Notice the 55-gallon drums allow access to the hull's interior.

Fig. 4-6B. The first of the outside layers of mesh going on and almost completed. Note the vertical spacing rods and how they are carefully bent over the keel.

The proportion is then 1.25; multiply all dimensions and offset figures by this conversion factor to obtain dimensions for the larger boat.

To save steps when enlarging or decreasing fractions, use Fig. 4-5. The table converts inches and fractions to decimal parts of a foot.

Assume that one portion of a hull frame is 7 1/8-in. long and the builder wants to enlarge it by 25 percent. First locate 1/8 in. on Fig. 4-5 and go across the page until directly under the 7 in. column. Where these two intersect will be the decimal of a foot: .5937 of a foot.

Then multiply .5937 by the previously calculated conversion factor: 1.25 x .5937 = .742125. Reversing the procedure will convert .742125 of a foot back into inches and fractions of a foot: 8 15/16 in., which is the new enlarged dimension. When converting, stay either over or under the nearest standard dimension as given on the chart and be consistent during calculations.

Open-Mold Method

The open-mold method is the fastest way to complete a hull. Adapted from the cedar mold method, the wood stringers that completely cover all station frames in the cedar mold method are left off. Only one or two stringers on each side of the hull are

Fig. 4-7A. Open-mold method, showing hull inverted. Notice horizontal spacer rods are overlapped so that the overlap is staggered to either the port or starboard sides.

Fig. 4-7B. Open-mold method, hull in upright position.

required to support the mesh. The open-mold method eliminates the long messy job of stripping out the wood on the inside when the hull has cured.

Start with the wood station frames, assembled and at the site ready for erection on the main supporting timbers. Secure them to the timbers, check the fairing and nail on the stringers. Figure 4-3 shows the station frames in place. Next start putting on the initial layer of wire mesh, simply laying it over the station frames and supporting stringers. When this is completed, start putting on the reinforcing bars, horizontal rods first and then the vertical rods. Wire these together at irregular intervals, making sure that they are well secured and will not move. Then put on the outer layers of mesh and start wiring everything together. A pair of needle-nose pliers can be used to pull the baling wire through from the inside to the outside. Push all wired ends into the center of the void.

The initial layer of mesh and the horizontal bars are shown in Fig. 4-6A; notice the vertical spacing rods in Fig. 4-6B. The open-mold method with the hull inverted is illustrated in Fig. 4-7A, and the hull in the upright position is shown in Fig. 4-7B.

Get the mallet out and start the fairing process. It shouldn't be too difficult. Make certain that all loose ends of the mesh are wired down.

The next step is plastering the hull; procedures and instructions for plastering are found in Chapter VI. It is important to follow the steps given in Chapter VII when curing the hull. When the hull has cured for the necessary time, remove the station frames; then roll the hull out and if it is inverted get it in the upright position. If the hull is a sailboat, now is the time to get the keel poured and the propeller shaft log and rudder installed. This is followed by the installation of tanks, deck fittings, etc. All deck fittings are put in place before plastering the deck.

Additional information on installing spacer rods, placing mesh, putting in tanks and deck fittings is given in this chapter.

Hull Frame Fabrication – Open Pipe Frame Method (Figs. 4-8A, B & C)

Tools Needed

1. Full size plans of: frame stations and stern stations
2. Pipe bending tool
3. Flexible ruler, trisquare
4. Hacksaw
5. Chalk, suitable files, etc.
6. String
7. Batten boards

Materials Needed

1. Sufficient lengths of pipe suitable for hull frames
2. Welding rods or arc welding rods

This portion of the hull must be correct, whether its lines are curved, straight, or "V" type. The final shape and fairing of the hull is dependent upon the accurate bending of the frames. The lofting of accurate full-size frame lines is essential.

Always start bending frames at one end and work toward the other end. If small diameter pipe is used, an electrician's bending dickey will be stout enough to do the job. Place several sticks over the full-length pattern of the hull frame then lay the pipe on the sticks. This prevents scratching out the pattern marks or lines. The bending of pipe frames is a slow, tedious job, and kinking the pipe while bending it must be avoided. A hydraulic bender, one of the portable, hand-pumped models, can be used to bend the pipe frames and the keel pipes. Avoid heating the pipes if at all possible, because extreme care is necessary to avoid kinking or over bending the pipe beyond the pattern. Making a series of bends close together, and checking often to see that the

Fig. 4-8A. Open pipe frame method.

Fig. 4-8B. Typical open pipe frame method. Horizontal rods being installed.

frame matches the pattern is the best procedure. This "patient" method plus experience is important when bending frames.

If the frames are going to be supported from overhead beams, then figure in the extra length and don't cut it off — simply weld another piece of pipe to it. Now is the time to mark each pair of frames with the L.W.L. marks so that this mark can be transferred later to the shed side. Tag each pair of hull frames for later use and make tags with the following information on them:

Station frame number — (No. 1 frame starts from the bow).

Right or left frame — (Looking from stern to bow).

Once the keel and stern and stern pieces have been fabricated, set up the frames and weld them to the keel, wire on several horizontal spacer rods at the top of the hull and weld the end frames at bow and stern. Then put in planks athwartships to keep the hull frames from being bent inward and proceed to start fairing the lines.

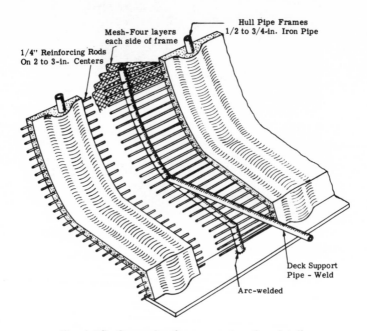

Fig. 4-8C. Open pipe frame construction details.

The open pipe frame method is ideally suited to the commercial builder who can build a series of permanent jigs upon which to bend the pipe frames to the various curves that are needed on each station. Once each station jig is made, heat the length of pipe and bend it on the jig, remove it and weld it to the keel section. The overall cost is quite low if a number of hulls are to be built.

Low capital investment in inventories and other equipment are excellent features of the open pipe frame system. A workable marine railway and a sturdy shed are the only major fixed cost items needed. A shore-side crane could eliminate the railway.

Floating docks are another prime item that can be manufactured at low cost, using a steel rod frame, welded on a jig, then installing mesh, rods, and the outer mesh. Then the mortar can be applied to the sides and ends. After the cement has started to set, turn the bottom up and cover it. Applications of open frame ferro-cement construction are endless, and the above use is mentioned as a further stimulation of ideas.

Keel Fabrication and Assembly

Tools Needed

1. Arc welder
2. Oxygen-acetylene welder
3. Hacksaw
4. Pipe support blocks (V-blocks)
5. Assorted "C" clamps
6. Assorted vise grip type of pliers
7. Assorted metal and wooden support timbers
8. Small electric bench grinder or hand grinder

Materials Needed

1. Enough pipe of varying sizes in sufficient length to fabricate keel
2. Arc welding rods and/or oxy-acetylene rods
3. Construction tie wire

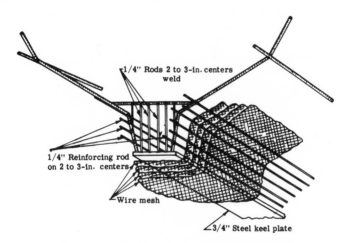

Fig. 4-9A. Hull section using steel plate keel.

There are two distinct and different methods to the assembly of the keel and both are excellent methods. They are:

The steel plate keel (Fig. 4-9A)

The pipe frame keel (Fig. 4-9B)

The steel plate keel lends itself to the sailboat that requires ballast. It is quite easy to fabricate with a minimum amount of time involved. A rather thick steel plate is used, normally about 1/2 to 3/4 in. thick. This plate can be cut in the widths called for in the hull plans. Some welding will be necessary to obtain the proper length.

The keel plate is put into place and the middle hull frames and fore and aft keel pipes are welded to it. After all hull frames are in place and welded, horizontal spacer rods are wired to hull frames (on one-foot centers). This ensures that frames will not be bent when hull is later inverted to the upright position. If hull is already upright, supporting rods are secured to hull frames and overhead beams. If the hull is kept upright, the ballast of heavy concrete is poured inside the keel proper and ferro-cement is added on the outside after a suitable wet-to-dry epoxy cement has been liberally applied. This initial pouring of the ballast has the advantage of stiffening the hull frames after setting.

Concrete is one of the least expensive materials that can be used for ballast. Extra heavy concrete is quite easy to mix and use, but smaller batches must be used.

Generally speaking, normal weights of sand and cement will weigh about 135 to 150 lbs. per cubic foot. To obtain heavy ballast concrete add steel punchings or scrap nuts and bolts. Even ball bearings that have been condemned could be used. A good ratio to use is two tons of steel to about three tons of concrete. The steel punchings are added to the mortar just prior to dumping the batch into the wheelbarrows or holding bay. (It is inadvisable to use a mortar/plaster pump with ballast mortar, especially when steel punchings are used.)

Builders who are unable to obtain steel punchings or other scrap iron, can order either one of two types of ore, called Barite and Magnetite. These ores are excellent radiation shields and are used in atomic reactors.

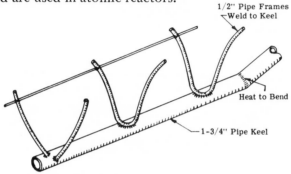

Fig. 4-9B. Single-pipe keel.

Ore brokers sell these ores to various manufacturers and local sand and gravel companies. Contact some of these concerns to obtain the going price and the address of a broker who would handle the order. Check the *Thomas Register* in the local library for firms that market Barite and Magnetite. Kaiser Sand and Gravel Corp., Oakland, California can give some information and help.

Another way of putting in ballast should be considered. Use normal weight concrete for ballast, but before starting to pour, place large-diameter clay or cement pipes vertically on the center line of the keel, say on one or 1 1/2-ft. centers, the entire length of the keel. Then, pour the normal weight mortar around these pipes. After curing, knock the protruding pipes down to the level of the poured ballast. Either before or after the hull is in the water, pour lead into the vertical pipes, starting from the center of gravity and working forward and aft. Having the hull in the water avoids lengthy mathematical calculations. One specific rule must be followed when pouring molten lead: *Ensure that all moisture is out of pipes before pouring molten lead.* Dangerous explosions can result if this rule is not followed.

The multi-pipe keel is simply a series of pipes welded together side-by-side to take the place of a conventional wooden keel. The keel is just a bit wider than its wooden counterpart, especially at the points where the hull frames are attached. Another type of pipe keel is made by using one long length of pipe that is simply welded to the bottom of the hull frames. See Fig. 4-9B. (This is done after the keel pipe is bent to shape and secured in an upright position.)

Careful layout and fitting procedures must be employed before the actual assembly and welding of the multi-pipe keel. First, lay out with chalk the actual size of the side, top and end views of the keel section. Then cut all pipes to length, grinding all ends to their proper curvature so that everything fits properly. Lay out and assemble, then tack-weld the two sides of the keel and clamp together and tack temporarily. Now check and recheck to ensure that the keel is faired right, nothing is out of plumb and it is of the correct length, etc. Proceed to weld the keel alternating from one side to the other, and, if arc welding, chip all slag off each weld.

When the keel is finished, place it in its proper place; weld hull frames to the keel. Tack-welding is called for here, since it may be necessary to bend or replace a frame if it does not fair up after all frames are put in. Check all L.W.L. marks on hull frames and transfer these marks to the side of the shed so these marks can be transferred to the ferro-cement hull when finishing time rolls around.

Horizontal Spacer Rod Installation (Fig. 4-10)

Tools Needed

1. Arc welder
2. Oxy-acetylene welder
3. Heavy duty electrician's pliers with cutters
4. Hacksaw and spare blades
5. Bolt cutters
6. Tie wire belt and holder
7. Large wooden and rubber mallets

Materials Needed

1. Arc welding rods and/or Oxy-acetylene rods
2. Tie wire, bailing wire or construction tie wire
3. Smooth reinforcing rod of various diameters, notably 1/4, 3/16, and 1/8 in. rod.

When the hull frames have been welded to the keel, bow, and stern, and frames have been attached to the overhead supporting beams, start putting on the 1/4, 3/16, or 1/8-in. horizontal spacer rods (Fig. 4-10), whichever the case may be. Keep all rods as straight as possible, taking care not to bend the rod when attaching it to the hull frames. A bent rod will show as a bulge or depression on the finished hull and these will be hard to correct. Bulges or depressions require a large amount of epoxy filler to correct the fault.

Spacing ranges from two-in. centers all the way to six-in. centers. This spacing depends on the hull thickness and type of spacer rod and mesh used, and on the number of layers used. Spacer bar centers should be established so that the inner and outer layers of mesh will not be pushed together when the plaster is applied.

Figure 4-10 shows the correct method of tieing the spacer rods to the hull frames for maximum strength and economical use of tie wire.

There are two approaches to joining spacer rods together. One method is to overlap on the side of the hull (at least a six to eight-in. overlap) and wrap with tie wire along the major part of the overlap. The second way is to weld the rods together. This is not recommended because of the possibility of warping either in or out. Rods should be welded to the stern and stern pipes, however, to give maximum strength. If an arc welder is unavailable, then bend the rods around the bow and continue on for a foot or so before tieing. Alternate this amount of overlap with greater rod overlap so that each row is staggered. This helps avoid a big bulge in any one spot on either side. The same applies to the stern section.

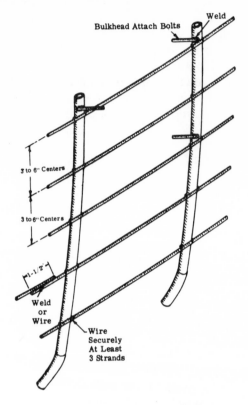

Fig. 4-10. Spacer rod installation.

After the horizontal rods are securely tied down the next step prior to applying mesh is to check alignment of the keel and also the frames, and finally to do any fairing necessary with the mallets mentioned. Make certain that there aren't any horizontal spacer bars that are pushed in, because these are most difficult to correct once the mesh is applied. Also, at this time get the thwartships bracing planks well secured so that the hull frames can't move in when working inside the hull.

Mesh Installation (Figs. 4-6 A & B)

Tools Needed

1. Mallets of assorted sizes, rubber and wood
2. Construction tie wire holder and belt
3. Heavy electrician's pliers with side cutters
4. Large sheet metal tin snips

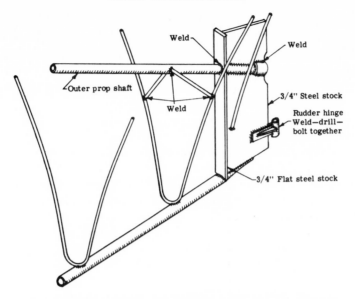

Weld

Weld

Outer prop shaft

Weld

3/4" Steel stock

Rudder hinge
Weld—drill—
bolt together

3/4" Flat steel stock

Fig. 4-11A. Rudder post and prop shaft installation prior to rod and mesh installation.

Fig. 4-11B. Engine prop shaft being fitted. Note that rudder opening is ready for rudder post to be installed and sealed.

Materials Needed

1. Mesh. First choice: 18 gauge, 1-in. opening, 3 or 4-ft. by 150-ft. lengths of mesh, enough to complete the hull.
   Second choice: 18 gauge, 1/2 in. open diamond opening, 3-ft. by 150-ft. lengths of mesh.
   Third choice: Plasterer's lath, 1/4-in. opening, 30-in. by 8-ft. lengths (if mortar/plaster pump is available).
2. Construction tie wire, as many rolls as needed to finish the job.

The first step in mesh installation is to unroll the mesh and double it over lengthwise to have two thicknesses. Start placing the mesh at the bow and let it hang down from the top of the hull and spot wire it into place. Overlap each successive layer by at least four to six inches, until reaching the stern and overlap this section. Also wire on the transom mesh. The next step is to fold the mesh under the keel up onto the sides of the hull and wire this up. Next the inside of the hull is done, and the same procedures followed.

Wiring now can start in earnest. This phase will be tedious and long. All overlaps must be tied down securely (Fig. 4-6B). This is best accomplished by using an in-and-out weave with a long piece of tie wire. In other parts of the mesh this method is also recommended, and the wire should be securely tied around the hull frames on the inside and the twisted end bent into the void. Get the mesh as taut as possible, so that when the cement plaster is applied, the two layers of mesh will not be pushed together. Wiring should be done at least every six or eight inches to get everything well secured.

When the mesh is on, fair out the hull once more. This is an important function and should be done carefully since irregularities might show up when the hull is finished.

Propeller Shaft, Integral Tanks, and Other Fittings

The drawing Fig. 4-11A shows rudder post and propeller shaft installations. Figure 4-11B illustrates the engine propeller shaft being fitted.

Integral tanks, Figures 4-12A, B,& C shouldn't be too difficult to construct. Careful planing procedures are a must when building integral tanks. If for any reason the tank is punctured, access cover plates must have openings large enough for the average person to get through and be so placed that the cover can be easily removed and put aside. Baffle plates (Fig. 4-12C) are an optional item if tanks are placed next to the keel section. Place baffle plates so that one can get to other areas of the tank if repairs are needed. Allow about 18 to 22 inches from the top of the baffle plate to the top of the tank, this will allow one to crawl to all areas of the tank for repairs, especially on the hull side of the tank. Interior tank finishing should be accomplished before the tank top is placed. Fabricate tank top separately and finish the underside, then place on top of tank. Use epoxy cement grout to seal top to sides of tank. This procedure will eliminate a messy upside down finishing of the underside of the tank. *Prior to entering any tank, insure that proper breathing devices are available and used,* most finishes are toxic, especially the epoxy finishes.

You may want to install the engine before starting on the deck. Engine motor mounts should have rods extending to all parts of the hull, with particular emphasis on extending the rods well down into the keel. Wire securely prior to placement of outer layers of mesh.

After these jobs have been done, start putting in the vertical and horizontal spacing rods for the decks and bulkheads, Figs. 4-13A, B, C & D. Always insure that there is a slight curve in the decks. The main reason is that a slightly curved deck will be much stronger than a flat one. Another is that rain water will naturally drain into the scuppers. It is advisable to use spacing rods on either 2-1/2" or 3" centers.

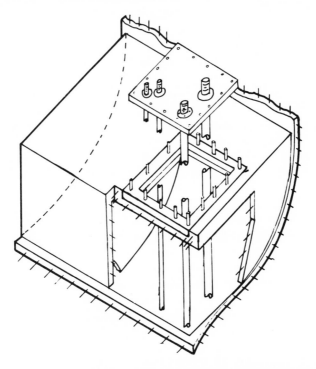

Fig. 4-12A. Tank cover, 3/4 inch steel. Note that threaded pipe flanges are welded or bolted to either side of cover plate for through pipe connections. Ensure that filler pipe extends within one inch of tank bottom.

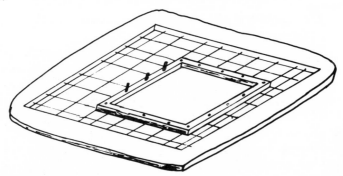

Fig. 4-12B. Tank gasket plate, 3/4 X 1-inch steel stock. Prior to placement of mesh, rods are arc-welded or wired to underside of plate. Place wood dowels in tapped holes before applying the mortar.

On superstructures, flat stock can be used for frames and reinforcing rods can be welded to the back side. For portholes, the mating frames with the glass is installed with a suitable watertight gasket and the whole thing bolted together with monel nuts and bolts. Use epoxy paint to keep the rust problems to a minimum.

For hulls that do not use vertical spacing rods, chain bearing plate reinforcements are recommended. Insure that rods are extended down and into keel sections. (See Fig. 4-16 for details.)

Hull stiffeners must be used on V-type hulls and on hulls that are slightly curved. Flat surfaces will not flex when the craft is underway if stiffeners are used. Spacing of

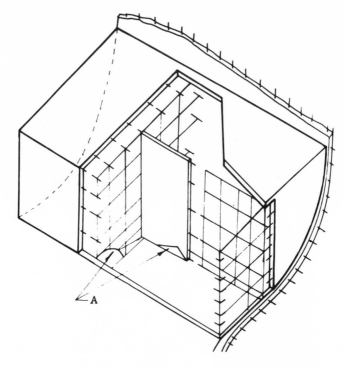

Fig. 4-12C. Integral tank baffle plate installation. A) Ensure that baffle plate drains are large enough for good fluid flow to lowest pick-up point of tank.

Fig. 4-13A. Deck and bulkhead rods attached to hull prior to mesh installation and application of mortar. Note curvature of deck.

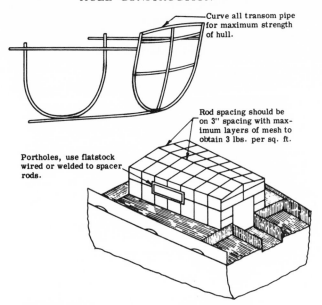

Curve all transom pipe for maximum strength of hull.

Rod spacing should be on 3" spacing with maximum layers of mesh to obtain 3 lbs. per sq. ft.

Portholes, use flatstock wired or welded to spacer rods.

Fig. 4-13B. Transom and superstructure details.

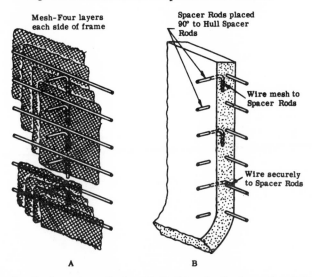

Mesh-Four layers each side of frame

Spacer Rods placed 90° to Hull Spacer Rods

Wire mesh to Spacer Rods

Wire securely to Spacer Rods

A   B

Fig. 4-13C. Bulkhead attachment methods. A) Bulkhead attachment rods before the placement of mortar; B) after the placement of mortar.

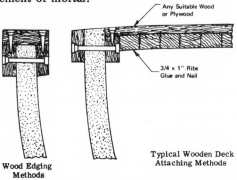

Any Suitable Wood or Plywood

3/4 x 1" Ribs Glue and Nail

Wood Edging Methods

Typical Wooden Deck Attaching Methods

Fig. 4-14. Wooden deck edging and attachment methods.

stiffeners range from 24″ to 36″. Figures 4-18 A & B show hull stiffeners. Remember hull stiffeners are important in any flat bottom or V-type hull that is broad beamed. When stiffeners are not used the hull life of a ferro-cement boat will be shortened.

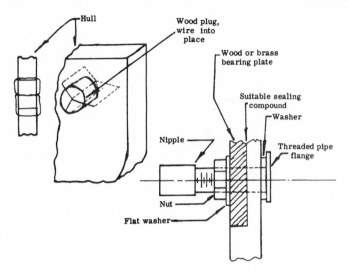

Fig. 4-15A. Through hull piping detail.

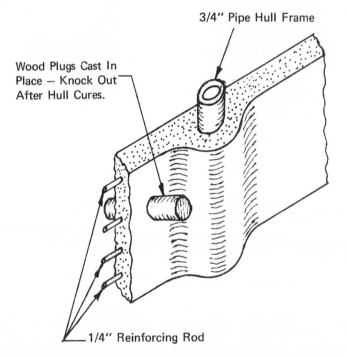

Fig. 4-15B. Wood plug used for drain and through hull fittings.

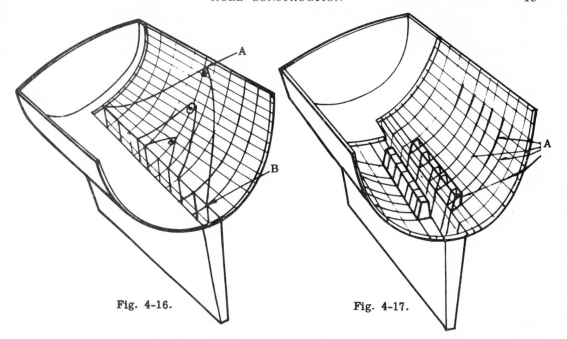

Fig. 4-16.   Fig. 4-17.

Fig. 4-16. Chain bearing plate reinforcement, recommended for hulls not using vertical spacing rods. A) Arc-weld bearing plate to rod, sparingly to avoid hull distortion. B) Extend rods down to and into keel section, wiring securely to spacer rods.

Fig. 4-17. Engine mount details prior to mesh installation. A) To prevent localized cracking of hull when diesel engines are installed, ensure that mounting rods extend from keel, up sides of hull, and fore and aft of hull. Wire securely to other hull support rods.

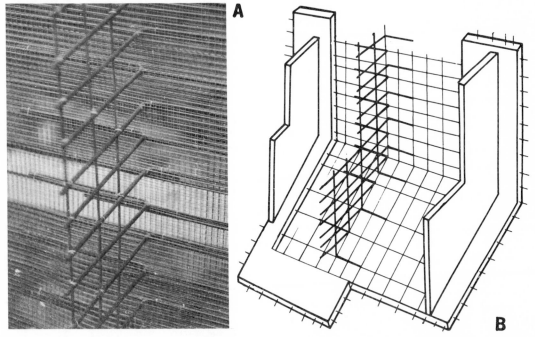

Fig. 4-18A. Hull stiffeners, used when "V" type or flat-bottomed type of hull is built, prior to covering with mesh.

Fig. 4-18B. Hull stiffeners, used when "V" or flat-bottomed hull form is constructed, prior to covering with mesh.

V

MIXING PROCEDURES

Survey all suitable sites around the construction and shed area, and place the mortar mixer in the best location. It will be advantageous if one side of the building area is on a slope or ledge. If the area is level and flat, a two-tier platform should be built. A large raised platform is necessary for the mixer and receiving tub to be above the height of the wheelbarrows used to transport the mortar, thus eliminating tiresome stooping and lifting by the temporary hod carriers. See Fig. 5-1.

The raised tier above and around the sides and back of the mortar mixer is for storage of the various ingredients, i.e., sand, aggregates, and pozzolans. Build a shelf or rack for the admixtures. The tier should be high enough so that the bags or boxes of ingredients can be pushed to the side and tilted into the mixer. Let gravity do the heavy work. Have sturdy boardwalks built so that there is an incline down to the hull platform for transportation of the mortar. Try to avoid upgrades.

Have good drainage under the platform, since the mixer will be rinsed off after each batch is mixed and discharged. A hose with a quick-release handle is a necessity and several buckets should be handy.

Allow sufficient room on the mixer platform for the operator to work and to store as many batches of mortar as convenient; usually around five complete batches will be sufficient. Have another level platform of the same height as the mixer platform where the main supply of cement and aggregates may be stored. This will facilitate use of a wheelbarrow or wagon for transporting the heavy materials to the mixer platform. Have suitable covers for protection against damp and rainy weather.

The mixing charts in this chapter show various water/cement ratios. This is to allow the builder to experiment *before* applying any mortar to the hull so that proper consistency and workability can be observed and applied to practice hull sections. In the engineering reports in Chapter X, a 0.35 water/cement ratio is recommended as the best ratio for general ferro-cement use. However, this may not be the optimum ratio for a particular hull, hence many ratios are listed. Try them and determine which is most suitable for your purposes.

The same is true for the sand/cement ratios. Going two steps over or under the 2:1 ratio when experimenting for actual use on the hull is recommended. Experiment with the other ratios for the experience gained in actually observing the results of the extreme ends of these ratios. If possible, send a few samples to a testing lab if more qualitative figures are desired. If admixtures are used, figure out *exactly* how much to use, since the amount will be minimal.

Absorption and surface moisture of aggregates should at this time be determined, so net water content can be figured and the correct batch weights calculated prior to bagging the sand. Workability and yield (strength) of the mortar can be radically affected if moisture is not checked at bagging and at the start of the mortar mixing phase.

If the sand (fine aggregates) is less than saturated it will absorb some of the previously figured mixing water. This will be about 3 percent or less by dry weight of sand, giving the mortar a stiff working consistency. Wet or damp aggregates carry water. This contributes to the plasticity (workability) of the mortar mix. Fine aggregates in this state will carry 10 to 12 percent by dry weight of sand. Assuming that the calculated moisture content is 8 percent, then the batch weight of the sand must be increased by 8 percent and the amount of mixing water reduced by a similar amount.

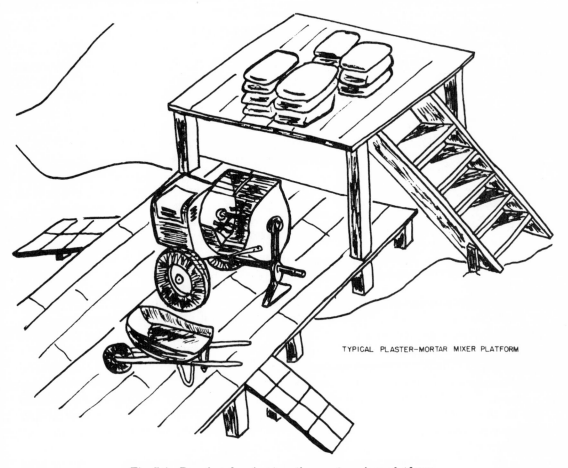

TYPICAL PLASTER-MORTAR MIXER PLATFORM

Fig. 5-1. Drawing showing two-tier mortar mixer platform.

The internal structure of a sand particle is made up of solid matter and voids that may or may not contain water. The four moisture conditions are as follows:

1. Oven dry: Fully absorbent.

2. Air dry: Dry at the particle surface, but containing some interior moisture; thus somewhat absorbent.

3. Saturated surface dry: Neither absorbing water from nor contributing water to the mortar mix.

4. Damp or wet: Containing an excess of moisture on the surface.

Bulking occurs when sand is damp and is shoveled or moved. The surface moisture around the sand particles holds the sand apart, causing an increase in volume. Bulking varies with moisture content and grading—fine sands bulk more than the medium and coarse sands. Since batching of sands by volume will give wide variations in sand ratios, proportioning by volume is not recommended for ferro-cement.

There are two simple testing methods to determine exact moisture content. The first is to dry a weighed sample of damp sand either on a hot plate, in an oven, or over an open fire. The percentage of moisture can be calculated from the weights before and after drying. The second method is to evaporate the moisture by burning alcohol. Place a weighed sample of damp sand in a shallow pan and pour alcohol over the sand (1/3 cup per pound). After the mixture has been stirred and spread in a thin layer, ignite the alcohol and keep burning until the sand is dry. After cooling, the sand is weighed and the percentage of moisture computed. When these methods are used to determine the free moisture, an adjustment should be made for the amount of water absorbed by the sand because only the free moisture becomes part of the mix water. This absorption then may be figured as 1 percent for average sand aggregates (fine). *Note:* For greater accuracy this figure (1 percent) may be determined by other methods as outlined in ASTM (American Society for Testing Materials) C127 and C128.

Now that the mixer area, boardwalks, mortar mixer, scales, materials, and water are in place, take a dry run to see that everything is within easy reach and that there is plenty of working room. Correct any obvious shortcomings before actually starting the plastering operation.

Now is the time to assemble the ingredients. Following is an example for the mixing ratios, etc.:

Water/cement ratio 0.35
Sand/cement ratio 2.1
Batch size to use 2 bags of cement per load;
                   4 94-lb. bags of sand per load

First acquire non-breakable, large-mouthed containers that can be marked with paint or permanent crayon. These level markings are to denote the proper amount of water for each batch of ingredients that go into the mixer. Usually three to four containers will have to be used to make up the total water requirements. Decide now to use either pounds or gallons of water per batch of mortar. Hold to this decision and be sure the man on the mortar mixer understands this point.

Assume that 20 two-bag batches of mortar will be needed. This means that at least two to three batches will be at the mixer and the rest close by on the storage platform, with the ingredients (aggregates) already weighed and bagged, ready to go onto the wheelbarrow.

On the storage platform have the area laid out so that paint lines show separate areas that will have the following: bags of cement; bags of aggregate (weighing the correct amount); bags of pozzolan (pre-sifted and proper weight). On the mix platform, have the liquid or powdered admixtures on a shelf with each batch in a separate box. After charging the mixer with all ingredients, put empty containers in a nearby box to keep them separate from the unused containers. This will aid in determining at a glance how many batches are left by counting the unused containers of admixtures. Again, make certain that the mix operator understands the system so as to avoid double mixing of the ingredients, which could be disastrous.

The bagging procedure will obviously call for suitable containers. The best and most inexpensive are the bags that the aggregate dealers get; they are new kraft paper cement bags. Obtain at least 80 to 100 of these bags, and 50 to 100 small plastic bags for the pozzolans and the powdered admixtures. Use a lever or beam type scale, such as doctors or grain dealers use. Measure the ingredients and make certain that the scale is accurate for the small powdered admixtures. One note on the pozzolans: before weighing, use a fine flour sifter to sift all the pozzolan. This removes any lumps and assures that the pozzolan will mix readily with the other ingredients. If possible, use plastic moisture-proof bags for the pozzolans to prevent future lumping.

Lightweight aggregates should not be weighed as the sand is weighed. Build a box that is one cubic foot in capacity and weigh the box on a set of scales. Record this figure, then fill the box with the lightweight aggregate, weigh it and subtract the weight of the box to obtain the weight of the aggregate. Put the aggregate in a large pan and place it in an oven to dry out completely. Weigh it again to see how much water was in the aggregate. Then add that much more aggregate to the original and subtract that much water from the mixing water. So, for a 2:1 sand/cement ratio, weigh out two boxes of lightweight aggregate, dry it, subtract twice the weight of the box and the weight of the water, add extra aggregates, and start batching out the aggregates into bags. Further information on batching of lightweight shale or clay aggregates may be obtained by writing to the companies listed in Chapter II.

If everything is at hand and the crew is ready, make certain again that the mixer operators adhere to the following steps when charging the mixer:

Step No. 1. Water — add most of it first
Step No. 2. Pozzolans
Step No. 3. Admixtures
Step No. 4. Cement
Step No. 5. Sand
Step No. 6. Water — add what is left from Step No. 1

Mix ingredients thoroughly, but do not overmix. Use a mix time of at least three minutes and not more than six minutes. Again it must be stressed: do not add extra water without measuring it into a graduated beaker and then observing how it will affect the workability. The mortar may become too wet. Also notice how it will affect the water/cement ratio and the ultimate strength. My advice is *not* to add extra water and to make certain that the mortar application crews understand the no-extra-water rule.

If mortar is left for any appreciable time on mortarboards, or anywhere waiting to be used, *discard it* and mix a new batch. The mixer operator should time his mixing, observing the rate of time it takes to deliver and apply the mortar by the crew members. This will help to eliminate the mixing and dumping of mortar that has partially set. Remember that the ultimate strength of the ferro-cement hull depends on many careful steps, from the placement of the mortar-mixer to the careful weighing of all the ingredients.

Schedule the crew so that everyone gets frequent breaks. Always have two or three men on breaks so that placement of mortar is always going on, even though part of the crew is resting. Pushing, lifting, and applying mortar is extremely hard work and mistakes always happen when people are tired and the "little things" slip by. Mistakes can be disastrous when mortar is being applied, especially so when it hardens.

British Gallons of Water Needed for:

Water/Cement Ratio	1/2-Bag Mix	1-Bag Mix	1-1/2-Bag Mix	2-Bag Mix
.35	1.75 Imp. Gal.	3.5 Imp. Gal.	5.25 Imp. Gal.	7.0 Imp. Gal.

Canadian Gallons of Water Needed for:

Water/Cement Ratio	1/2-Bag Mix	1-Bag Mix	1-1/2-Bag Mix	2-Bag Mix
.35	1.35 Imp. Gal.	2.7 Imp. Gal.	4.05 Imp. Gal.	5.4 Imp. Gal.

Metric Liters of Water Needed for:

Water/Cement Ratio	1/2-Bag Mix	1-Bag Mix	1-1/2-Bag Mix	2-Bag Mix
.35	7.7 Ltr.	15.4 Ltr.	23.1 Ltr.	30.8 Ltr.

U.S. Gallons of Water Needed for:

Water/Cement Ratio	1/2-Bag Mix	1-Bag Mix	1-1/2-Bag Mix	2-Bag Mix
.35	1.75 U.S. Gal.	3.5 U.S. Gal.	5.25 U.S. Gal.	7.0 U.S. Gal.

Australian Gallons of Water Needed for:

Water/Cement Ratio	1/2-Bag Mix	1-Bag Mix	1-1/2-Bag Mix	2-Bag Mix
.35	1.45 Imp. Gal.	2.9 Imp. Gal.	4.35 Imp. Gal.	5.8 Imp. Gal.

Note: Pozzolith 7 and 8A reduce water content by 12%. This is by weight (kg. or lbs.) to cement, then, converted to gallons or to liters as the case may be.

Fig. 5-2. Modified water mixing chart: To be used only when water-reducing agents are used.

| | 1 Bag Cement 112 lbs. | |
	1 Imperial Gallon 10 lbs.	
Water/Cement Ratio by Weight Per Bag	Lbs. of Water Per Bag	Imp. Gal. of Water Per Bag
.30	33.60	3.36
.31	34.72	3.47
.32	35.84	3.58
.33	36.96	3.69
.34	38.08	3.80
.35	39.20	3.90
.36	40.32	4.00
.37	41.48	4.14
.38	42.56	4.25
.39	43.68	4.36
.40	44.80	4.40
.41	45.92	4.50
.42	47.04	4.70
.43	48.16	4.80
.44	49.28	4.90
.45	50.40	5.00
.46	51.52	5.10
.47	52.64	5.20
.48	53.76	5.30
.49	54.88	5.40
.50	56.00	5.60

Fig. 5-3. Basic British Weight and Measure Charts for: Water, Sand, and Admixtures.

Imperial Gallons Needed for:

Water/Cement Ratio	1/2-Bag Mix	1-Bag Mix	1-1/2-Bag Mix	2-Bag Mix
.30	1.7	3.4	5.1	6.8
.31	1.75	3.5	5.25	7.0
.32	1.8	3.6	5.4	7.2
.33	1.85	3.7	5.6	7.4
.34	1.9	3.8	5.7	7.6
.35	1.95	3.9	5.9	7.8
.36	2.0	4.0	6.0	8.0
.37	2.05	4.1	6.1	8.2
.38	2.15	4.3	6.5	8.6
.39	2.2	4.4	6.6	8.8
.40	2.25	4.5	6.7	9.0
.41	2.3	4.6	6.9	9.2
.42	2.35	4.7	7.0	9.4
.43	2.4	4.8	7.2	9.6
.44	2.45	4.9	7.4	9.8
.45	2.5	5.0	7.5	10.0
.46	2.55	5.1	7.7	10.2
.47	2.65	5.3	8.0	10.6
.48	2.7	5.4	8.1	10.8
.49	2.75	5.5	8.2	11.0
.50	2.8	5.6	8.4	11.2

Fig. 5-4. British Water Mixing Chart.

Pounds of Water Needed for:

Water/Cement Ratio	1/2-Bag Mix	1-Bag Mix	1-1/2-Bag Mix	2-Bag Mix
.30	16.80	33.60	50.40	67.20
.31	17.36	34.72	52.08	69.44
.32	17.92	35.84	53.76	71.68
.33	18.48	36.96	55.44	73.92
.34	19.04	38.08	57.12	76.16
.35	19.60	39.20	58.80	78.40
.36	20.16	40.32	60.48	80.64
.37	20.74	41.48	62.22	82.96
.38	21.28	42.56	63.84	85.12
.39	21.84	43.68	62.52	87.35
.40	22.40	44.80	67.20	89.60
.41	22.96	45.92	68.88	91.84
.42	23.52	47.04	70.56	94.08
.43	24.08	48.16	72.24	96.32
.44	24.64	49.28	73.92	98.56
.45	25.20	50.40	75.60	100.80
.46	25.76	51.52	77.28	103.04
.47	26.32	52.64	78.96	105.28
.48	26.88	53.76	80.64	107.52
.49	27.44	54.88	82.33	109.76
.50	28.00	56.00	84.00	112.00

Fig. 5-5. British Water Mixing Chart.

Pounds of Sand Needed for:

Sand/Cement Ratio	1/2-Bag Mix	1-Bag Mix	1-1/2-Bag Mix	2-Bag Mix
1.30:1 or .76	73.7	147.4	221.1	294.8
1.40:1 or .71	78.9	157.8	236.7	315.6
1.50:1 or .66	84.8	169.6	254.4	339.2
1.60:1 or .61	91.8	183.6	275.4	367.2
1.80:1 or .56	100.0	200.0	300.0	400.0
1.95:1 or .51	109.9	219.8	329.7	439.6
2:1 or .50	112.0	224.0	336.0	448.0
2.20:1 or .46	121.7	243.5	362.2	487.0
2.45:1 or .41	136.7	273.4	410.1	546.8
2.75:1 or .36	155.6	311.2	466.8	622.4
3:1 or .31	180.6	361.2	541.8	722.4
3.80:1 or .26	215.4	430.8	646.2	861.6

Fig. 5-6. British Sand Mixing Chart.

Pounds of Extra Fines Needed for:

Type of Extra Fines	1/2-Bag Mix	1-Bag Mix	1-1/2-Bag Mix	2-Bag Mix
Pozzolans	7.84	15.68	23.52	31.36
Diatomaceous Earth	0.84	1.68	2.52	3.26

Pounds of Admixtures Needed for:

Type of Agents	1/2-Bag Mix	1-Bag Mix	1-1/2-Bag Mix	2-Bag Mix
Pozzolith 8*	0.149	0.298	0.447	0.596
Pozzolith 8A**	0.149	0.298	0.447	0.596
MV-BR*** Resin	4.47 cc	8.94 cc	13.41 cc	17.88 cc

* Retarding agent only.
** Combination retarding and air-entrainment agent.
*** Air-entrainment agent only, single-strength Vinsol Resin.

Fig. 5-7. British Admixtures Mixing Chart.

1 Canadian Bag Cement 87.5-lbs.
1 Imperial Gallon 10.0-lbs.

Water/Cement Ratio by Weight Per Bag	Lbs. of Water Per Bag	Imp. Gal. of Water Per Bag
.30	26.25	2.6
.31	27.13	2.7
.32	28.00	2.8
.33	28.87	2.87
.34	29.75	2.9
.35	30.62	3.0
.36	31.50	3.1
.37	32.37	3.2
.38	33.25	3.3
.39	34.12	3.4
.40	35.00	3.5
.41	35.88	3.58
.42	36.75	3.6
.43	37.62	3.7
.44	38.50	3.8
.45	39.37	3.9
.46	40.25	4.0
.47	41.12	4.1
.48	42.00	4.2
.49	42.87	4.29
.50	43.75	4.3

Fig. 5-8. Basic Canadian Weight and Measure Charts for Water, Sand, and Admixtures.

Water Cement Ratio	Imperial Gallons of Water Needed for:			
	1/2-Bag Mix	1-Bag Mix	1-1/2-Bag Mix	2-Bag Mix
.30	1.3	2.6	3.9	5.2
.31	1.35	2.7	4.0	5.4
.32	1.4	2.8	4.2	5.6
.33	1.43	2.87	4.3	5.7
.34	1.45	2.9	4.4	5.8
.35	1.5	3.0	4.5	6.0
.36	1.55	3.1	4.6	6.2
.37	1.6	3.2	4.8	6.4
.38	1.65	3.3	4.9	6.6
.39	1.7	3.4	5.1	6.8
.40	1.75	3.5	5.2	7.0
.41	1.79	3.58	5.3	7.1
.42	1.8	3.6	5.4	7.2
.43	1.85	3.7	5.5	7.4
.44	1.9	3.8	5.7	7.6
.45	1.95	3.9	5.8	7.8
.46	2.0	4.0	6.0	8.0
.47	2.05	4.1	6.1	8.2
.48	2.1	4.2	6.3	8.4
.49	2.14	4.28	6.4	8.5
.50	2.15	4.3	6.45	8.6

Fig. 5-9. Canadian Water Mixing Chart.

Pounds of Water Needed for:

Water/Cement Ratio	1/2-Bag Mix	1-Bag Mix	1-1/2-Bag Mix	2-Bag Mix
.30	13.13	26.25	39.38	52.50
.31	13.57	27.13	40.70	54.26
.32	14.00	28.00	42.00	56.00
.33	14.44	28.87	43.31	57.74
.34	14.38	29.75	44.13	59.50
.35	15.31	30.62	45.93	61.24
.36	15.75	31.50	47.25	63.00
.37	16.20	32.37	48.56	64.74
.38	16.63	33.25	49.88	66.50
.39	17.06	34.12	51.18	68.32
.40	17.50	35.00	52.50	70.00
.41	19.94	35.88	53.82	71.76
.42	18.38	36.75	55.13	73.50
.43	18.81	37.62	56.43	75.24
.44	19.25	38.50	57.75	77.00
.45	19.69	39.37	59.06	78.74
.46	20.13	40.25	60.38	80.50
.47	20.60	41.12	61.72	82.24
.48	21.00	42.00	63.00	84.00
.49	21.44	42.87	64.31	85.76
.50	21.88	43.75	65.63	87.50

Fig. 5-10. Canadian Water Mixing Chart.

Pounds of Sand Needed for:

Sand/Cement Ratio	1/2-Bag Mix	1-Bag Mix	1-1/2-Bag Mix	2-Bag Mix
1.30:1 or .76	57.55	115.13	172.68	230.26
1.40:1 or .71	61.62	123.24	184.86	246.48
1.50:1 or .66	66.15	132.29	198.43	264.48
1.60:1 or .61	71.72	143.44	215.16	286.88
1.80:1 or .56	78.13	156.25	234.37	312.50
1.95:1 or .51	85.79	171.57	257.36	343.14
2:1 or .50	87.50	175.00	262.50	350.00
2.20:1 or .46	95.11	190.11	285.33	380.44
2.45:1 or .41	105.40	210.81	316.21	421.62
2.75:1 or .36	121.50	243.10	364.60	486.20
3:1 or .31	135.61	271.23	406.83	542.46
3.80:1 or .26	168.26	336.53	504.74	673.06

Fig. 5-11. Canadian Sand Mixing Chart.

Pounds of Extra Fines Needed for:

Type of Extra Fines	1/2-Bag Mix	1-Bag Mix	1-1/2-Bag Mix	2-Bag Mix
Pozzolans	6.46	12.91	19.36	25.82
Diatomaceous Earth	0.66	1.31	2.00	2.62

Pounds of Admixtures Needed for:

Type of Agents	1/2-Bag Mix	1-Bag Mix	1-1/2-Bag Mix	2-Bag Mix
Pozzolith 8*	0.116	0.232	0.348	0.464
Pozzolith 8A**	.116	.232	.348	.464
MV-BR*** Resin	3.485 cc	6.97 cc	10.460 cc	13.94 cc

* Retarding agent only.
** Combination retarding and air-entrainment agent.
*** Air-entrainment agent only, single-strength Vinsol Resin.

Fig. 5-12. Canadian Admixtures Mixing Chart.

	1-Metric Bag Cement, 50 Kg. 1-Standard Liter, 1 Kg.	
Water/Cement Ratio by Weight Per Bag	Kg. of Water Per Bag	Ltr. of Water Per Bag
.30	15.0	15.0
.31	15.5	15.5
.32	16.0	16.0
.33	16.5	16.5
.34	17.0	17.0
.35	17.5	17.5
.36	18.0	18.0
.37	18.5	18.5
.38	19.0	19.0
.39	19.5	19.5
.40	20.0	20.0
.41	20.5	20.5
.42	21.0	21.0
.43	21.5	21.5
.44	22.0	22.0
.45	22.5	22.5
.46	23.0	23.0
.47	23.5	23.5
.48	24.0	24.0
.49	24.5	24.5
.50	25.0	25.0

Fig. 5-13. Basic Metric Weight and Measure Charts for: Water, Sand, and Admixtures.

Liters of Water Needed for:

Water Cement Ratio	1/2-Bag Mix	1-Bag Mix	1-1/2-Bag Mix	2-Bag Mix
.30	7.5	15.0	22.5	30.0
.31	7.75	15.5	23.25	31.0
.32	8.0	16.0	24.0	32.0
.33	8.25	16.5	24.75	33.0
.34	8.5	17.0	25.5	34.0
.35	8.75	17.5	26.25	35.0
.36	9.0	18.0	27.0	36.0
.37	9.25	18.5	28.75	37.0
.38	9.5	19.0	28.5	38.0
.39	9.75	19.5	29.25	39.0
.40	10.00	20.0	30.0	40.0
.41	10.25	20.5	30.75	41.0
.42	10.5	21.0	31.5	42.0
.43	10.75	21.5	32.25	43.0
.44	11.0	22.0	33.0	44.0
.45	11.25	22.5	33.75	45.0
.46	11.5	23.0	34.5	46.0
.47	11.75	23.5	35.25	47.0
.48	12.0	24.0	36.0	48.0
.49	12.25	24.5	36.75	49.0
.50	12.50	25.0	37.5	50.0

Fig. 5-14. Metric Water Mixing Chart.

Kilograms of Water Needed for:

Water/Cement Ratio	1/2-Bag Mix	1-Bag Mix	1-1/2-Bag Mix	2-Bag Mix
.30	7.5	15.0	22.5	30.0
.31	7.75	15.5	23.25	31.0
.32	8.00	16.0	24.00	32.00
.33	8.25	16.5	24.75	33.0
.34	8.50	17.0	25.5	34.0
.35	8.75	17.5	26.25	35.0
.36	9.0	18.0	27.0	36.0
.37	9.25	18.5	28.75	37.0
.38	9.5	19.0	28.5	38.0
.39	9.75	19.5	29.25	39.0
.40	10.0	20.0	30.0	40.0
.41	10.25	20.5	30.75	41.0
.42	10.5	21.0	31.5	42.0
.43	10.75	21.5	32.25	43.0
.44	11.0	22.0	33.0	44.0
.45	11.25	22.5	33.75	45.0
.46	11.5	23.0	34.5	46.0
.47	11.75	23.5	35.25	47.0
.48	12.0	24.0	36.0	48.0
.49	12.25	24.5	36.75	49.0
.50	12.50	25.0	37.5	50.0

Fig. 5-15. Metric Water Mixing Chart.

Kilograms of Sand Needed for:

Sand/Cement Ratio	1/2-Bag Mix	1-Bag Mix	1-1/2-Bag Mix	2-Bag Mix
1.30:1 or .76	32.90	65.78	98.67	130.00
1.40:1 or .71	35.21	70.42	105.63	140.84
1.50:1 or .66	37.87	75.75	113.62	151.50
1.60:1 or .61	40.60	81.18	121.80	162.40
1.80:1 or .56	45.55	90.10	136.65	182.20
1.95:1 or .51	49.00	98.00	147.00	196.00
2:1 or .50	50.00	100.00	150.00	200.00
2.20:1 or .46	54.35	108.70	163.05	217.40
2.45:1 or .41	60.98	121.95	182.92	243.90
2.75:1 or .36	69.06	138.12	207.18	276.24
3:1 or .31	80.65	161.29	241.93	322.58
3.80:1 or .26	96.19	192.38	288.57	384.76

Fig. 5-16. Metric Sand Mixing Chart.

Kilograms of Extra Fines Needed for:

Type of Extra Fines	1/2-Bag Mix	1-Bag Mix	1-1/2-Bag Mix	2-Bag Mix
Pozzolans	3.16	6.31	9.47	12.62
Diatomaceous Earth	.375	.750	1.125	1.50

Kilograms of Admixtures Needed for:

Type of Agents	1/2-Bag Mix	1-Bag Mix	1-1/2-Bag Mix	2-Bag Mix
Pozzolith 8*	.066	.133	.194	.266
Pozzolith 8A**	.066	.133	.194	.266
MV-BR*** Resin	4.31 cc	8.62 cc	12.93 cc	17.24 cc

* Retarding agent only.
** Combination retarding and air-entrainment agent.
*** Air-entrainment agent only, single-strength Vinsol Resin.

Fig. 5-17. Metric Admixtures Mixing Chart.

1 Bag Cement, 94.0 lbs.
1 U.S. Gallon, 8.33 lbs.

Water/Cement Ratio by Weight Per Bag	Lbs. of Water Per Bag	U.S. Gal. of Water Per Bag
.30	28.20	3.4
.31	29.14	3.5
.32	30.08	3.6
.33	31.02	3.7
.34	31.96	3.8
.35	32.90	3.9
.36	33.84	4.1
.37	34.78	4.2
.38	35.72	4.3
.39	36.66	4.4
.40	37.60	4.5
.41	38.54	4.6
.42	39.48	4.7
.43	40.42	4.8
.44	41.36	5.0
.45	42.30	5.1
.46	43.24	5.2
.47	44.18	5.3
.48	45.12	5.4
.49	46.06	5.5
.50	47.00	5.6

Fig. 5-18. Basic U.S. Weight and Measure Charts for Admixtures, Sand, and Water.

U.S. Gallons of Water Needed for:

Water/Cement Ratio	1/2-Bag Mix	1-Bag Mix	1-1/2-Bag Mix	2-Bag Mix
.30	1.7	3.4	5.1	6.8
.31	1.75	3.5	5.25	7.0
.32	1.8	3.6	5.4	7.2
.33	1.85	3.7	5.55	7.4
.34	1.9	3.8	5.7	7.6
.35	1.95	3.9	5.85	7.8
.36	2.05	4.1	6.15	8.2
.37	2.1	4.2	6.3	8.4
.38	2.15	4.3	6.45	8.6
.39	2.2	4.4	6.6	8.8
.40	2.25	4.5	6.75	9.0
.41	2.3	4.6	6.9	9.2
.42	2.35	4.7	7.05	9.4
.43	2.4	4.8	7.2	9.6
.44	2.45	4.9	7.35	9.8
.45	2.5	5.0	7.5	10.0
.46	2.55	5.1	7.65	10.2
.47	2.5	5.3	7.8	10.4
.48	2.7	5.4	8.1	10.6
.49	2.75	5.5	8.25	10.8
.50	2.8	5.6	8.4	11.2

Fig. 5-19. U.S. Water Mixing Chart.

Pounds of Water Needed for:

Water/Cement Ratio	1/2-Bag Mix	1-Bag Mix	1-1/2-Bag Mix	2-Bag Mix
.30	14.10	28.20	42.30	56.40
.31	14.57	29.14	43.71	58.28
.32	15.04	30.08	45.12	60.16
.33	15.51	31.02	46.53	62.04
.34	15.98	31.96	47.94	63.82
.35	16.45	32.90	49.35	65.80
.36	16.95	33.89	50.84	67.78
.37	17.39	34.78	52.17	69.56
.38	17.86	35..72	53.58	71.44
.39	18.33	36.66	54.99	73.32
.40	18.80	37.60	56.40	75.20
.41	19.27	38.54	57.81	77.08
.42	19.74	39.48	59.22	78.96
.43	20.21	40.42	60.63	80.84
.44	20.68	41.36	62.04	82.72
.45	21.15	42.30	63.45	84.60
.46	21.62	43.24	64.86	86.48
.47	22.09	44.18	66.27	88.36
.48	22.56	45.12	67.68	90.24
.49	23.03	46.06	69.09	92.12
.50	23.50	47.00	70.50	94.00

Fig. 5-20. U.S. Water Mixing Chart.

Pounds of Sand Needed for:

Sand/Cement Ratio	1/2-Bag Mix	1-Bag Mix	1-1/2 Bag Mix	2-Bag Mix
1.30:1 or .76	62.00	124.00	186.00	248.00
1.40:1 or .71	66.00	132.00	198.00	264.00
1.50:1 or .66	71.00	142.00	213.00	284.00
1.60:1 or .61	74.00	154.00	292.00	308.00
1.80:1 or .56	84.00	168.00	252.00	336.00
1.95:1 or .51	92.00	184.00	276.00	368.00
2:1 or .50	94.00	188.00	282.00	376.00
2.20:1 or .46	102.00	204.00	306.00	408.00
2.45:1 or .41	114.50	229.00	343.50	458.00
2.75:1 or .36	130.50	261.00	391.00	522.00
3:1 or .31	145.00	291.00	436.50	582.00
3.80:1 or .26	180.00	361.00	541.50	722.00

Fig. 5-21. U.S. Sand Mixing Chart.

Pounds of Extra Fines Needed for:

Type of Extra Fines	1/2-Bag Mix	1-Bag Mix	1-1/2-Bag Mix	2-Bag Mix
Pozzolans	7.00	14.00	21.00	28.00
Diatomaceous Earth	0.705	1.41	2.11	2.82

Pounds of Admixtures Needed for:

Type of Agents	1/2-Bag Mix	1-Bag Mix	1-1/2-Bag Mix	2-Bag Mix
Pozzolith 8*	0.125	0.25	0.375	.50
Pozzolith 8A**	0.125	0.25	0.375	.50
MV-BR*** Resin	3.75 cc	7.50 cc	11.25 cc	15.00 cc

*   Retarding agent only.
**   Combination retarding and air-entrainment agent.
*** Air-entrainment agent only, single-strength Vinsol Resin.

Fig. 5-22. U.S. Admixtures Mixing Chart.

1 U.S. Bag Cement, 94 lbs.
1 Imperial Gallon,   10 lbs.

Water/Cement Ratio by Weight Per Bag	Lbs. of Water Per Bag	Imp. Gal. of Water Per Bag
.30	28.20	2.8
.31	29.14	2.9
.32	30.08	3.0
.33	31.02	3.1
.34	31.96	3.2
.35	32.9	3.3
.36	33.84	3.4
.37	34.78	3.5
.38	35.72	3.6
.39	36.66	3.7
.40	37.60	3.8
.41	38.54	3.85
.42	39.48	3.9
.43	40.42	4.0
.44	41.36	4.1
.45	42.30	4.2
.46	43.24	4.3
.47	44.18	4.4
.48	45.12	4.5
.49	46.06	4.6
.50	47.00	4.7

Fig. 5-23. Basic Australian Weight and Measure Chart for Water.

VI

PLASTERING AND FINISHING

In preparation for plastering, it is wise to set aside a final day to inspect every inch of the hull for loose rods, mesh, etc. Check all frames or station molds and make sure that they are still firmly secured to the main support timbers. If the hull is on rollers or pipe, check again that it is secure.

Next, see that all the necessary ingredients — cement, aggregates and admixtures, mixing equipment, wheelbarrows and delivery walks — are ready to go. Plastering is perhaps the most critical phase of the hull construction. Use a check sheet for these items. A mistake discovered later could prove to be disastrous.

The last step is to brief the crew of helpers who will be mixing or delivering mortar and putting the mortar into the hull. Emphasize the fact that no extra water is to be added to mortar and that old or partially set mortar is to be discarded.

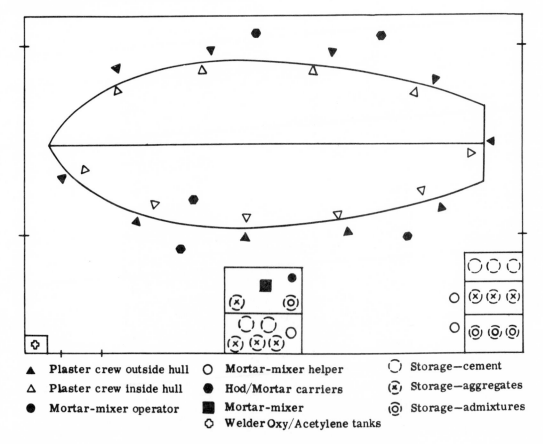

▲ Plaster crew outside hull	○ Mortar-mixer helper	◌ Storage—cement
△ Plaster crew inside hull	● Hod/Mortar carriers	⊗ Storage—aggregates
● Mortar-mixer operator	▪ Mortar-mixer	◎ Storage—admixtures
	♂ Welder Oxy/Acetylene tanks	

Fig. 6-1. A suggested shop and plastering team layout.

Fig. 6-2. Mortar being hoisted to the plastering team.

Fig. 6-3. Plastering team applying mortar to transom corners.

The diagram in Fig. 6-1 shows one example of a typical shop and plastering team layout. The movement of mortar from mixer to the plastering team via the mortar carriers requires the coordinated efforts of all members. In Fig. 6-2 the mortar carriers are shown hoisting mortar to the plastering crew. A continuous supply of mortar is essential when plastering the hull.

Now is the time to pull out several test slabs that have been previously made and have the crew go through the operation, from mixing to applying the mortar, including delivering the actual-sized mortar loads. This session will enable each person to evaluate the operations. The team will then be ready to proceed with the job when the actual day of plastering arrives.

Plastering should be started from the bottom and worked upward. Keep in mind that corners and other hard-to-reach places should be done first (see Figs. 6-3 & 6-4). Then spread out to the easier-to-reach places on the hull.

Fig. 6-4. Application of mortar in keel section.

The use of a mortarboard (a square board with a handle) is highly recommended. Mortar can be transferred from a bucket to the board and then to the mesh by means of the trowel in a quick fashion. Simultaneous movements of the mortarboard and the trowel toward each other will place the most mortar on the trowel. Make certain that a new mortar container is used each time, or at least every other time, when mortar is delivered to your area.

When vibrators are used on ferro-cement hulls, considerable quantities of mortar will fall through the hull membrane if the vibrator is held in one spot too long. The vibrator should be used briefly, about four to seven seconds or less. The amount of vibration in one spot can be gauged by the texture and surface movement of the mortar and by the appearance of the mortar where it contacts and flows around spacer bars and mesh. Frequently the operator can judge by the sound and by the feel of the vibrator in his hands. When overvibration occurs (assuming that the mortar has not fallen through the hull membrane), the surface of the mortar appears very wet and will consist of a layer of mortar containing practically no coarse or medium sands. If a dry mix is used, this condition should not happen.

As mentioned earlier, start placement of mortar from the bottom and work up, placing vibrator in the mortar at an angle and slowly withdrawing it. To avoid missing any part of the applied mortar, there should be some overlapping of the area previously warped. In shallow or inaccessible places of the hull, consolidations can be obtained by using the vibrator in a horizontal position in or adjacent to the placed mortar.

Most curved sections of the hull can be considered as sloping, so when placing mortar on a slope, always start at the bottom so that compaction is increased by weight of newly applied mortar. Vibration will then consolidate the mortar. If mortar is placed at the top of a slope, it tends to pull apart when vibration applied below starts a downward flow of mortar.

Vibrators cannot be used when plastering the underside of decks from below, unless there is suitable form work under the deck membrane. If the underside of the deck has been placed by hand and has set, vibration may be used when applying mortar to the topside of the deck since the mortar will not vibrate through. Allow at least two to three weeks for underside of deck mortar to cure before placing top layer of mortar.

Plastering the Underside of Decks

Plastering the underside of the decks should be tried at the practice session. Work only a small area and apply the mortar with a short scraping or pushing motion. A point to remember is the mesh will support the mortar. It is tricky, but always try to have a full trowel of mortar — it seems to stick to the underside for some reason. Practice makes perfect, so just start. Complete penetration is not necessary at this time, since more mortar will be applied from the top later.

To get a maximum of penetration, put the mortar into the mesh and then press it in with a hard pushing or scraping motion. It is important to keep moving and maintain a steady placement of mortar. Leave the professional finishing to the plasterer, your main job is to get a complete penetration of the mortar into the mesh. (See Fig. 6-5.) A

Fig. 6-5. Mortar being forced through the hull membrane from the inside, ensuring complete penetration.

certain amount of set is required before mortar takes a finish, so the plasterer can complete the finishing aspect of the job at the proper time.

Plastering is probably the most fun of the whole operation, but can be a problem unless a common sense approach is applied. The practice of measuring sand, cement and water with a shovel, or the attitude that a bit of extra water is okay and no need to clean up till the job is done, will not build a first-rate ferro-cement hull. A well-planned building area, plus thorough checking of the hull at every phase, proper maintenance of equipment, careful measurement of materials, quick delivery of proper-sized mortar loads, and thorough application of mortar by the crews are essential in producing an excellent ferro-cement hull.

Fig. 6-6. Final finishing of hull by professional plasterers.

The finishing operation presents some difficulty. Make arrangements for at least two plasterers, one coming on after the other, so that continuity is achieved for that extra smooth finish. Figure 6-6 shows the final finishing of the hull by professional plasterers. When the mortar has set to a "green" condition the hand- or machine-grinding stones can be used.

Finishing the Marco Polo

The *Marco Polo* is a 55-ft., double-ended, three-masted schooner designed by L. Francis Herreshoft (Fig. 6-7). This boat was built by Richard Muenzer (see Foreword) using the open mold method.

The hull was plastered by a crew of five professional plasterers, who applied the mortar with a mortar/plaster pump to assure that complete penetration of the metal plasterer's lath was achieved in a minimum amount of time. Placement and final finishing took one day. The hull was then cured for the full 28 days by spraying with water.

As mentioned earlier, the use of the 1/4-in. metal plasterer's lath is not recommended for the builder who will be placing mortar by hand. Unless a large plastering crew and the necessary mixing capacity are available the mortar will set faster than it can be forced through the hull membrane. The minimum size openings of metal plasterer's lath to use is the 1/2-in. or 3/4-in., for hand application of the mortar. Builders who place mortar by hand should use 18-gauge chicken wire with the 1-in. octagon-shaped openings as this is easy to obtain and mortar is easily forced through the hull membrane with a trowel.

Fig. 6-7. After curing, the hull is turned right side up, painted, and now ready for completion of decks, tanks, ballast (lead), and propeller shaft.

Materials Used and Their Cost

Cement:	48 bags (high early strength, Type III)
Aggregates:	96 bags (one bag weighs 94 lbs)
High Tensile Steel Rod:	10,670 feet, 1/4-in. diameter
Plasterer's Metal Lath:	30 bundles (10 sheets 30 in. x 96 in. to a bundle)
Plywood:	30 sheets (4' x 8' x 3/4" thick)
Equipment:	1 mortar/plaster pump

The total cost of materials and labor for the *Marco Polo* was surprisingly low considering that the hull was 55 feet in length. The cost was $1,500, labor of the builder and his wife excepted.

If full-time effort were put into the building of the hull, it could be completed in six to eight weeks.

Finishing without a Professional Plasterer

Finishing without the aid of a professional plasterer is indeed a task that has to be approached with determination and "intestinal fortitude."

The advice to build several ferro-cement panels with which to practice is even more applicable when trying to obtain a passable amount of knowledge in finishing procedures. Have several panels placed at various angles to the vertical to simulate the curvature of the hull. Also try a couple of panels overhead.

Practice with one panel at a time. Have a helper act as a timekeeper noting the time started and time finished when applying mortar and the time the actual finishing started. Observe how fast the mortar takes a set and can still be finished smooth with a trowel. The main thing here is to document every step and observation. Since temperature and moisture affect setting time, take accurate temperature readings, and humidity readings, if at all possible; number each practice panel so comparison with later panels can be made. A scientific approach eliminates some of the guesswork in the timing of the finishing operation.

A smooth finish can be achieved with a trowel when the mortar is still in a wet or early plastic state. Small edges will tend to be erased if smoothed over during this particular stage. If the mortar is troweled too much in one place, however, the fine aggregates tend to be drawn to the surface. Holding the trowel so that the edges do not dig in on either side is of importance.

Timing is vital. Try to work when the mortar is just about right to take a "mechanic's finish" (as the plasterer would say), or a finish that is smooth without trowel marks being made when moving over to the adjoining area to be finished. This state passes quite quickly, and this is where the advice to keep moving starts to pay off. Practice on trial panels, and try to learn to recognize this particular set of the mortar by experience, as well as from the recorded time trials.

Now assume that a finished panel or two have several trowel marks running in different directions on the surface — other than that, the finish is reasonably smooth. Carefully observe the setting of the mortar. When it is set and looks and feels crumbly when a piece is rubbed between the fingers, get the damp sponges ready to go. The trowel marks can be rubbed out with a circular motion. This will, however, roughen up the surface, and it will have to be finished off with a cement-finishing stone.

Concrete stones, which are rather coarse and are designed expressly for finishing concrete, are obtainable from equipment dealers who cater to the building industry. The Norton Abrasive Company handles them, as does the Stow Manufacturing Company. Finish grinding may be done by hand or by power grinder. This is usually done in the green state about 24 hours after plastering, when the mortar has not fully set and is not cured and hard. At this time, the mortar should be easy to grind, yet stout enough not to be damaged. Finishing after the hull has cured is a tedious, slow job, as compared to finishing during the green state.

An important factor that helps put a good finish on a hull is that of mixing consistent batches of mortar time after time. This is one variable that can be controlled and used as a base from which to recognize all the other signs that will indicate when the right time is approaching for the finishing operation.

Finishing is an acquired art and is only learned from experience. That means lots of practice prior to the finishing of the actual hull.

VII

CURING

Ferro-cement hull sections are extremely "thin", averaging one inch thick, so curing constitutes one of the major factors in achieving the proper strength of the ferro-cement. Watertightness, surface appearance, and ultimate strength are dependent on the very early stages of the curing process.

Improper curing will result in high shrinkage, cracks, spalling, and flaking. It will also negate all previous efforts that went into the construction of the hull. Protective waterproof coatings will not cure or hold together a badly cured ferro-cement hull.

Proper curing does two very important things. First, it retains sufficient moisture within the concrete to permit complete hydration of the cement. Second, curing stabilizes temperatures at the level required to insure that the chemical hydration is completed. Ideal initial curing is achieved when the concrete is kept at 70°F. and moist for a minimum of 28 days. The first three days are the most important; remember that concrete stops curing if allowed to dry out, and subsequent rewetting does not restart the curing process. Once curing is stopped, that's it, and the strength gained at that point is all that is retained.

Evaporation occurs very quickly in thin hull sections as opposed to a slab of concrete that is some six inches thick. Wind and humidity affect the rate of evaporation and can be a problem for ferro-cement builders in hot, dry areas.

Curing methods will normally consist of the use of several types of materials. They are: water, burlap, chemical membrane compounds, tar paper and plastic sheeting.

Water is sprayed over the entire area of the hull, inside and out. The spraying system can consist of a series of pipes with spray nozzles attached to them. Even shower heads are suitable, as long as the entire hull area is covered. Fogging nozzles do the same thing as the spray heads, except that they put out a very fine mist, as opposed to a spray. A fine mist is advantageous and recommended for the early stages of curing to prevent possible erosion from too coarse a spray. Wind breaks are a must if the wind prevents the spray from reaching all points of the hull.

Before the hull is plastered, place tapered wooden plugs (see Fig. 4-15B) through and as near the bottom of the hull as possible. These plugs can then be removed after the first day of curing, and will then allow excess spray water to drain from the inside of the hull. Remember that at least *three weeks* of curing is a *must* before attempting to place bulkheads *or* decks *or* before moving the hull.

Burlap bags are one of the most efficient materials to use for curing the hull. The bags are sewn into large sheets, laid and then tied on the outside of the hull, and draped on the inside of the hull (if hull is upright). These burlap sheets are then kept wet. This method keeps the direct rays of the sun off the curing concrete, thus reducing the evaporation of water from the hull.

Chemical membrane compounds have now become the building industry's favorite. They are inexpensive and quick to use. They come in black, white and grey colors. Two drawbacks of membrane compounds are mentioned. The first is that the hull should not be exposed to direct sunlight when membrane compounds have been used. Secondly, if a protective waterproof finish is to be applied to the outside and inside of the hull, then the membrane must be removed. (This is discussed further in the next chapter.)

Tar paper represents another method of retaining the moisture, but it should not be used unless a definite spraying schedule is adhered to. The drawbacks here are that the tar paper must be removed every time the hull is sprayed and tar paper can also leach out petroleum and stain the hull. Use this method *only* if nothing else is available.

Plastic sheeting is new to the construction industry and is quite suitable for ferro-cement curing (see Fig. 7-1). It is sold in varying thicknesses and in 100-ft. rolls

Fig. 7-1. Plastic sheeting used for covering the hull while curing. Note alternate steel pipe scaffolding for hull support and work platforms.

with up to 32-ft. widths. Its big advantage is that one of these sheets will cover a typical hull. This sheeting is lightweight, non-absorptive and mildew resistant. Plastic sheeting will last for about four to five months before the action of the sun's rays deteriorates the surface of the plastic. If at all possible, do not use clear or black plastic sheeting, since heat absorbed by the sun's rays will markedly increase the temperature of the concrete. A white opaque plastic sheet is best, and it should be ordered well ahead of time to insure that it will be on hand when needed.

A hothouse effect can be achieved by covering the hull area with plastic sheeting and forming it into a bubble with air pressure from a window exhaust fan placed in an opening in the sheeting. A very fine fogging nozzle can be installed inside and hooked up to a timer so that water is sprayed or fogged onto the hull automatically. This is ideal if the builder cannot be there around the clock to see that the hull is kept moist. A trip to a local plumber or greenhouse will be helpful in obtaining a timer that will be suitable. Compare the purchase or rental price of the timer to that of hiring someone to turn the sprayers on and off, or to the cost of leaving the water running day and night.

Hot-Weather Curing Procedures

Hot-weather curing of ferro-cement creates two very important problems. One is excessive evaporation, and the second is excessive heat in the freshly mixed and placed mortar. This build-up of heat will speed up the "set" of the mortar. This is where retardants come into play. They delay the time it takes for the mortar to set for about 30 to 45 minutes in addition to the estimated setting-up time of the mortar.

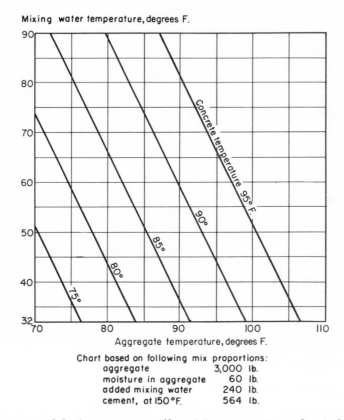

Chart based on following mix proportions:

aggregate	3,000 lb.
moisture in aggregate	60 lb.
added mixing water	240 lb.
cement, at 150°F.	564 lb.

Fig. 7-2. Temperature of fresh concrete as affected by temperature of materials. Although this chart is based on the mixture shown, it is reasonably accurate for other typical mixtures.

Minimum temperature for implementing hot-weather curing techniques is 85°F., or less if the wind is blowing. Try to start with cool materials. If possible, keep all materials stored in the shade or in a cool shed or garage. Provide cover over the top and sides of the hull to reduce the temperature of the reinforcing rods and mesh. A quick spray with water prior to applying mortar will help cool down things. Erect wind breaks if there are daily winds that come up and the hull is out in the open. If the wind *is* stronger than usual, have the previously mentioned burlap sheets prewetted and put over the freshly placed mortar, and remove them as the plasterer finishes each particular section.

Schedule the mixing and placing of mortar so that everything is in its place and everyone knows just what his or her job is going to consist of throughout the day. Be firm; stick to a predetermined schedule if it looks as if it has merit. The plasterer will be an immense help at this stage. The builder is paying him, so use him to the fullest. Do not allow the mixer to mix the mortar too long; the friction of the mixing action tends to increase the temperature of the mortar and makes for a stiffer mix, which is much more difficult for the crew to apply. In some cases it will become necessary to add extra water for workability, but this just reduces the strength of the mortar.

Remember that several water/cement ratios are given in the mixing charts in Chapter V. They can be used for prior experimentation to help determine just what the best water/cement ratio will be. This is the time to start a series of trial batches. Keep working them until a stiff batch is obtained, and then add a measured amount of water to get the proper workability. Then check the new water/cement ratio on the mixing charts to see that the strength originally wanted has not been exceeded or lost. Water retardants can be used here also to see what can be achieved. Note that a maximum water/cement ratio of .49 or .50 is the limit for good watertight concrete. In short, practice before the final placement of mortar.

The cooling of concrete materials is, of course, the best way of maintaining low concrete temperatures (Fig. 7-2). One or more of the materials may be cooled prior to mixing. The average specific heat (heat units required to raise the temperature of one pound of material 1°F.) of the solid material in concrete (cement and aggregates) may be assumed to be 0.22 Btu per pound per degree F., compared to 1.0° for water. This shows generally the effect of the temperature of each ingredient on the final temperature of the concrete. Although the temperature mixing charts shown in this chapter are based on the particular mix given, they are reasonably accurate for most ordinary mixtures. The purists and other slide rule devotees use the following general formula.*

$$T = \frac{0.22 \, (T_a \, W_a + T_c \, W_c) + T_f \, W_f + T_m \, W_m}{0.22 \, (W_a + W_c) + W_f + W_m}$$

In the formula T is the temperature in degrees F. of the fresh concrete. T_a, T_c, T_f, and T_m are temperature in degrees F. of the aggregates, cement, free moisture in aggregates, and added mixing water, respectively (usually $T_a = T_f$). W_a, W_c, W_f, and W_m are weight in pounds of the aggregates, cement, free moisture in aggregates, and added mixing water, respectively.

Of all the ingredients used in concrete, water is the easiest to cool, and is the most effective coolant pound for pound, for lowering temperature of concrete. Water used for mixing should be drawn from a cool source and stored in the shade. Pipes and storage tanks should be buried, insulated, or shaded so that water temperatures will be maintained at their lowest practicable point. It may even help to paint all pipes and tanks white. Crushed ice can also be used to reduce concrete temperatures and is more effective than water. As the cement and aggregates are cooled, the temperature of the ice and water melting from it consequently is raised. One pound of ice in melting absorbs 144 Btu; however, one pound of water heated one degree F. absorbs "only" 1 Btu. (For instance, one pound of ice heated from 32° to 73°F. absorbs 185 Btu, while one pound of water absorbs only 40-Btu when its temperature is raised from 33° to 73°F.) Hence, if 75 lbs. of ice per cubic yard were used in a concrete mix with a temperature of 90°F., the temperature would drop to about 75°F. Note that the amount of water and ice used must not exceed the total requirements for mixing water.

When ice is used, the formula for temperature of the fresh concrete is modified as follows:

$$T = \frac{0.22 \, (T_a \, W_a + T_c \, W_c) + T_f \, W_f + T_m \, W_m - 112 \, W_i}{0.22 \, (W_a + W_c) + W_f + W_m + W_i}$$

*All formulas and graphs in this chapter have been reprinted, with permission, from *Design and Control of Concrete Mixtures,* Portland Cement Association, Eleventh Edition, 1968.

where **W** is the weight, in pounds, of the concrete, and **Wi** is the weight, in pounds, of ice.

Air-entrainment of concrete is also affected by extremely hot weather. At high temperatures, additional air-entraining agents are necessary. Consult the manufacturer of the air-entrainment agent for the exact temperature range and *exact higher dosages*. These will vary from one manufacturer to another.

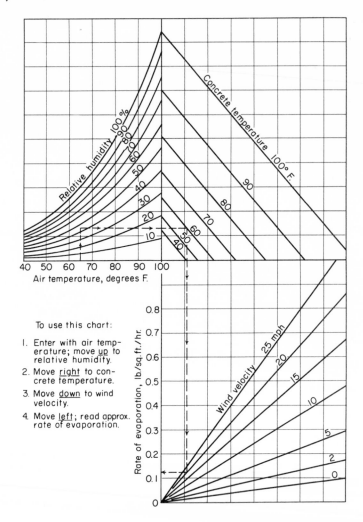

Fig. 7-3. Effect of concrete and air temperatures, relative humidity, and wind velocity on the rate of evaporation of surface moisture from concrete.

Repeating some of these factors, wind and humidity play major roles insofar as curing of ferro-cement hulls is concerned (Fig. 7-3). A high temperature, along with a moderate wind and low humidity, tends to push up concrete temperature and the rate of evaporation. Once again exercise caution when it comes to curing the hull; frequent wettings are safer than those spread over longer periods of time. This is especially so if the wind suddenly comes up and the hull isn't due to be sprayed until two hours later. Corners and edges are the first to dry out, so watch out for this, and base the spraying schedule on keeping these areas wet. Then the hull will cure properly. In order to calculate just how hard the wind is blowing, refer to the Beaufort Wind Scale.

Cold-Weather Curing Procedures

For those builders who reside in the "cold country," there are certain steps to take to get that ferro-cement hull done in the winter and launched in early spring.

The ideal temperature for curing is 70°F. and the minimum curing temperature is 50°F. The effect of low temperature is to slow down the curing process. All chemical hydration (curing) ceases at 40°F. and below.

The plastic mortar must be protected against freezing and this danger exists until the degree of saturation has been sufficiently reduced by the withdrawal of mixing water involved in hydration (or until the concrete has taken its final "set").

Low temperatures require less mixing water to achieve a workable mix. The result of this is to achieve a higher ultimate compressive strength after curing. Concrete of low slump is especially desirable for cold weather work. At minimum temperatures, evaporation is slowed and this tends to minimize bleeding, which helps to speed up finishing operations on the hull.

The Portland Cement Association has conducted tests on different curing temperatures using separate portions of one batch of concrete as a control factor. The mix data follow:

Type I Cement

Water/Cement ratio 0.43
Slump . . . . 2 to 4 in.
Air Content 4.6%

Temperature	Compressive Strength at 7 days	Compressive Strength* at 365 days
40°F.	about 40%	120%
55°F.	about 60%	135%
73°F.	about 75%	119%

*All specimens cured at 73°F. after 28 days.

Figure 7-4.

Thus concrete placed at or slightly above the minimum curing temperature will gain significantly higher strengths than will a similar concrete placed and cured at higher temperatures.

For successful cold-weather curing (Fig. 7-5), the first step is to erect a suitable

Line	Condition of Placement and Curing		Thin Sections	Moderate Sections (i. e., keel or ballast)
1.	Minimum Temp. fresh concrete	Above 30°F.	60°F.	55°F.
2.	"As Mixed" for weather indicated,	0 to 30°F.	65°F.	60°F.
3.	degree F.	Below 0°F.	70°F.	65°F.
4.	Minimum temperature fresh concrete, "As Placed," degree F.		55°F.	50°F.
5.	Maximum allowable "gradual" drop in temperature throughout first 42 hours after end of protection, degrees F.		50°F.	40°F.

Fig. 7-5. Recommended concrete temperatures for cold weather construction. Adapted from Recommended Practice for Cold Weather Concreting (American Concrete Institute 306-66).

weatherproof cover over the hull and associated working platforms. Also needed are suitable openings for heating ducts and exhaust ducts. The inside air temperature should be maintained at over 50°F. Of course fuel costs will be a consideration if temperatures are maintained at a very high level for any length of time. Actually, the higher temperatures are only needed when mortar is being applied and finishing operations are being conducted; then the temperature can be reduced to the lower levels until curing is finished; after that a gradual drop in temperature to that of the outside ambient air can be allowed.

In order to obtain a workable temperature of the concrete or mortar (Fig. 7-5), heat one or all of the ingredients. Concrete produces internal heat, but most of this heat is lost while transporting the mix to the work site or hull, especially if mixed outside the

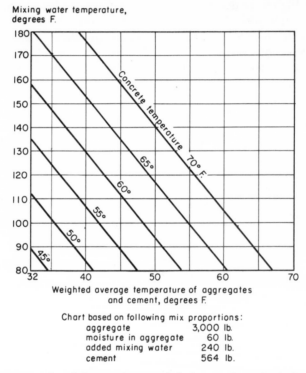

Chart based on following mix proportions:
aggregate   3,000 lb.
moisture in aggregate   60 lb.
added mixing water   240 lb.
cement   564 lb.

Fig. 7-6. Temperature of mixing water needed to produce heated concrete of required temperature. Although this chart is based on the mixture shown, it is reasonably accurate for other typical mixtures.

enclosed shed in extremely cold weather. Figure 7-6 shows the various mortar temperatures that should be achieved after pouring from the mixer. It is not necessary to have concrete with temperatures in excess of 70°F. If temperatures are above 32°F. it is not necessary to heat the aggregates. However, at temperatures well below freezing it is recommended that the aggregates be heated, with a maximum temperature not to exceed 150°F. The heating of aggregates can be something of a chore, and a couple of old restaurant or home liquid-propane-gas fired stoves are necessary for this job.

Water is the easiest ingredient to heat, and even a small gas-fired stove or burner can heat copious quantities of water in a relatively short time. The heat stored by water is some five times as much heat as that stored by solid materials. The cold-weather heating chart for the various ingredients that make up concrete (Fig. 7-5) shows the various effects of different temperatures of the ingredients, which all affect the concrete temperature. This chart is based on the foregoing formula.

Note that if the weighted temperature of the aggregates and cement is above 32°F., the proper mixing water temperature for the required concrete temperature can be selected from the chart. This range of concrete temperatures corresponds with the recommended values shown on lines 1, 2 and 3 of Fig. 7-5.

Another note of explanation for the cold-weather heating chart is that the maximum water temperature only goes to 180°F. The reason for this is that water heated above this temperature might possibly cause a flash set of the cement.

When water and/or aggregates are heated above 100°F., they should be placed in the mixer first. This will cause a temperature drop, which should not be more than to 80°F. In really cold weather, if the weighted average temperature of the cement and aggregates is below the 36°F. mark and the desired temperature is in the 70°F. range, then the aggregates must be heated in order to keep the water temperature below 180°F. to prevent a flash set.

Addition of moisture while cold-weather curing is a must, especially if dry, forced air is used to heat the shed. Steam is ideal, or a large bucket of water being boiled will generally take care of the moisture problem. If oil-fired heaters are being used inside, *allow for adequate ventilation* of the exhaust gases.

In extremely cold weather it is essential to maintain an even temperature throughout the shed, from floor to ceiling.

Hull curing time should be a full 28 days, although three days should be more than enough for the concrete to get its permanent set. Finally, check the corners and edges of the hull for drying out and freezing. These areas freeze first and, if desired, thermometers may be placed at these points, firmly taped to the hull with insulation placed on the air side. They will give a fair indication of how hot or cold the hull gets.

VIII

PROTECTIVE FINISHES

There are innumerable types of protective finishes for ferro-cement hulls, both inside and outside. The need for finishing is somewhat debatable if the hull is to be kept only in fresh water. Finishes are recommended for salt water exposure and the epoxy resin finishes are best, and easy to use. The use of anti-fouling paint is necessary and must be applied twice a year. This is all that needs to be done to the hull, effecting a saving on long-term hull maintenance.

Interior tankage for sewage and fuel tanks should have protective covering as a matter of course. Consult the tables for the appropriate type of finish. Remember that the correct surface preparation procedures are to be followed and will result in a surface that will take the specified finish quickly and easily.

The following material is reprinted with permission from the Portland Cement Assn.; *Effect of Various Substances on Concrete and Protective Treatments. Where Required*, 1968.

(Continued on following pages)

Protective Treatments

1. Magnesium fluosilicate or zinc fluosilicate: The treatment consists generally of three applications. Either of the fluosilicates may be used separately, but a mixture of 20 percent zinc and 80 percent magnesium appears to give the best results. For the first application, 1 lb. of the fluosilicate crystals should be dissolved in 1 gal. of water; about 2 lb. of crystals per gallon of water are used for subsequent applications.

The solution may be applied efficiently with large brushes for vertical surfaces and mops for horizontal areas. The surfaces should be allowed to dry between applications (about three or four hours are generally required for absorption, reaction, and drying). Care should be taken to brush and wash the surface with water shortly after the last application has dried to remove incrusted salts; otherwise white stains may be formed.

Treatment with fluosilicates reduces dusting and hardens the surface by chemical action. It increases resistance to attack from some substances but does not prevent such attack. With poor-quality concrete, the treatment is not effective.

Concrete surfaces to be treated with fluosilicates should not contain integral water-repellent agents because these compounds will prevent penetration of the solution. Hardeners should not be used when paints are to be applied because they result in poor adhesion of many coatings. Also, the hardened surfaces are difficult to etch properly.

2. Sodium silicate (commonly called water glass): Commercial sodium silicate is about a 40 percent solution. It is quite viscous and must be diluted with water to secure penetration, the amount of dilution depending on the quality of the silicate and permeability of the concrete. Silicate of about 42.5 deg. Baumé gravity diluted in proportions of 1 gal. with 4 gal. of water makes a good solution. Two or three coats should be used. For tanks and similar structures, progressively stronger solutions are often used for the succeeding coats.

Each coat should be allowed to *dry thoroughly* before the next one is applied. On horizontal surfaces it may be liberally poured on and then spread evenly with mops, brooms, or brushes. Scrubbing each coat with stiff fiber brushes or scrubbing machines and water *after it has hardened* will assist penetration of the succeeding application. The treatment increases resistance to attack from some substances but does not prevent such attack.

3. Drying oils: Two or three coats of linseed, tung (China wood), or soybean oils may be used as a protective treatment. Boiled linseed oil dries faster than the raw oil and is the most commonly used.

The concrete should be well cured and at least 14 days old before the first application. If this is not possible, the concrete should be neutralized by applying a solution consisting of 3 oz. of zinc chloride and 5 oz. of orthophosphoric acid (85 percent phosphoric acid) per gallon of water. Brushed on the concrete, the solution should be allowed to dry for 48 hours and then any crystals that have formed on the surface should be removed by light brushing. This solution should not be used on prestressed concrete. Sometimes a magnesium fluosilicate treatment is also applied to harden the surface before the oil treatment.

The oil treatment may be applied with mops, brushes, or spray and the excess removed with a squeegee before the oil gets tacky. It is not necessary to build up a heavy surface coating as penetration of the oil into the surface is desirable. Diluting the oil with turpentine or kerosene up to a mixture of equal parts gives better penetration for the first coat; subsequent coatings may be diluted less. Careful heating of the oil to 150 deg. F. or so and hot application to a warm surface are also helpful in securing better penetration. Each coat must dry thoroughly for at least 24 hours before the next application. Drying oils tend to darken the concrete.

4. Coumarone-indene: Available in grades from dark brown to colorless, this synthetic resin is soluble in xylol and similar hydrocarbon solvents and should be powdered to

Protective Treatments—Cont.

aid dissolving. A solution consisting of about 6 lb. of coumarone-indene per gallon of xylol with ½ pint of boiled linseed oil makes a good coating. Two or more coats should be applied to fairly dry concrete. The coatings have a tendency to yellow on exposure to sunlight but this yellowing does not seem to affect the protective properties.

5. Styrene-butadiene: Styrene-butadiene copolymer resins are supplied in various medium-strength solvents, some faster drying than others. Three coats are generally recommended, with the first coat thinned for better penetration. Twenty-four hours should elapse between coats, and a delay of 7 days is necessary for thorough drying before the coated surface is placed in service. These coatings tend to yellow under the influence of sunlight.

Decorative styrene-butadiene coatings are widely marketed as latex paints. They are usually not satisfactory for protection against chemical attack because latex paints generally do not form sufficiently impermeable films.

6. Chlorinated rubber: This treatment consists of a trowel-applied or sprayed coat of heavy consistency mastic up to 1/8 in. thick, or multiple coats brushed or sprayed on to a thickness of up to 10 mils. A minimum of 5 mils is recommended for chemical exposure. A single brush coat will vary from about 1 to 2 mils, depending on consistency, while a single spray coat usually varies from 0.7 to 1.0 mils.

In general, concrete should age for two months before treatment. The concrete may be damp but not wet, as excessive moisture may prevent adequate bond. It is usually necessary to thin the first coat, using only the producer's recommended thinner (other thinners may be incompatible). A coating dries tack-free in an hour, but a 48-hour delay is recommended between coats.

This treatment is odorless, tasteless, and nontoxic. Its strong solvents, however, may lift and destroy previously painted and aged coatings of oil or alkyd base.

7. Chlorosulfonated polyethylene (Hypalon): Four coats of about 2 mils each and an appropriate primer are normally recommended to eliminate pinholes. Thinning is not usually required, but to reduce viscosity for spray application the producer's recommended thinner should be used up to a limit of 10 percent. Each coat dries dust-free within 10 to 20 minutes and the treatment cures completely in 30 days at 70 deg. F. and 50 percent relative humidity. A fill coat of grout or mortar is required as the paint film will not bridge voids in the concrete surface. Moisture on the surface may prevent good adhesion.

These coatings are high in material cost and require trained applicators. They are not used where less expensive coatings are adequate.

8. Vinyls: Of the vinyls available, polyvinyl chloride, polyvinyl chloride-acetate, and polyvinylidene chloride are the ones used extensively in corrosion control. The resins are soluble only in strong solvents. Due to the high viscosity of the resins, only solutions of low solids content can be made and multiple coats are therefore required for adequate film thickness. Vinyls should generally be applied to dry surfaces by spray as their fast drying (30 minutes) makes brush application difficult.

Vinyl chloride coatings make good top coatings for vinyl chloride-acetate and others, but they themselves do not adhere well directly to concrete. Polyvinyl acetate latex copolymers are widely available as decorative coatings but, like other latexes, they are usually inferior to the solvent-system coatings for chemical resistance.

9. Bituminous paints, mastics, and enamels: Asphalt or coal tar coatings may be applied cold (paints and mastics in cutback or emulsion form) or hot (mastics and enamels). Two coats are usually applied to surface-dry concrete: a thin priming coat to ensure bond and a thicker finish coat. The priming solution is of thin brushing consistency and should be applied so as to cover the surface completely; any uncoated spots should be touched up. When the primer has dried to a tacky state, it is ready for the finish coat. Multiple coats should be applied at right angles to each other to secure continuity and avoid pinholes.

Emulsions are slower drying, more permeable, and less protective than the other coatings. Cutbacks and emulsions, if not completely cured, can impart odor or flavor to materials with which they are in contact. The producer's recommendations on service and application temperatures should be strictly observed.

Bituminous mastics may be applied cold or heated until fluid. Cold mastics are cutbacks or emulsions containing finely powdered siliceous mineral fillers, asbestos fibers, or bitumen-coated fabrics to form a very thick, pasty, fibrous mass. This mass increases the coating's resistance to flowing and sagging at elevated temperatures and to abrasion. Thin mastic layers, about 1/32 in. thick, are troweled on and allowed to dry until the required thickness has been obtained. Hot mastics usually consist of about 15 percent asphaltic binder, 20 percent powdered filler, and the remainder sand, graded up to 1/4-in. maximum size. They should be poured and troweled into place in layers 1 in. or more in thickness.

Enamels should be melted, stirred, and carefully heated until they reach the required application temperature. If an enamel is heated above the producer's recommended temperature, it should be discarded. If application is delayed, the pot temperature should not be allowed to exceed 375 deg. F. When fluid, it should be applied quickly over tacky cutback primer as it sets and hardens rapidly.

10. Polyester: These resin coatings are two- or three-part systems consisting of polyester, peroxide catalyst, and

possibly a promoter. The amount of catalyst must be carefully controlled because it affects the rate of hardening. The catalyst and promoter are mixed separately into the polyester. Fillers, glass fabrics, or fibers used to reduce shrinkage and coefficient of expansion compensate for brittleness of resin and increase strength.

Coatings with 2- to 3-hour pot life generally cure in 24 to 36 hours at 75 deg. F. Shorter cure times require reduced pot life because of high heats of reaction. Coatings are sensitive to changes in temperature and humidity during the curing period. Some coatings can be applied to damp surfaces and at temperatures as low as 50 deg. F. The alkali resistance of some polyesters is limited. It is recommended that trained applicators apply the coatings.

11. Urethane: These coatings may be one- or two-part systems. There are two types of the one-part system: moisture-cured and oil-modified. The coatings that cure by reacting with moisture in the air must be used on dry surfaces to prevent blistering during the curing period. Oil-modified coatings dry by air oxidation and generally have the lowest chemical resistance of the urethane coatings.

Two types of the two-part system are also available: catalyzed and polyol-cured. Catalyzed coatings have limited pot life after mixing and cure rapidly. For polyol-cured coatings, the mixture is well stirred and allowed to stand for about 1/2 hour before use; it should have a pot life of about 8 hours. Polyol-cured coatings are the most chemically resistant of the urethane coatings but require the greatest care in application.

All urethane coatings are easily applied by brush, spray, or roller. For immersion service in water and aqueous solutions, it may be necessary to use a primer and the urethane producer should be consulted. Satisfactory cure rates will be attained at relative humidities of 30 to 90 percent and temperatures between 50 and 100 deg. F. Lower temperatures will retard rate of cure.

The principal disadvantages of urethane coatings are the very careful surface preparation needed to ensure adhesion

Protective Treatments—Cont.

and the difficulty in recoating unless the coating is sanded. Multiple coats should be used and an inert filler added if air voids are present on the concrete surfaces (the coatings are unable to span air voids).

12. Epoxy: These coatings are generally a two-package system consisting of epoxy resin—which may be formulated with flexibilizers, extenders, diluents, and fillers—and a curing agent. The coating properties are dependent on the type and amount of curing agent used. The common curing agents suitable for room temperature curing are amines, polyamines, amine adducts, polyamides, polysulfides, and tertiary amines.

The single-package coatings are epoxy esters that are generally inferior to the two-package epoxies in chemical resistance. They require an alkali-resistant primer and are not recommended for immersion service. Some epoxy formulations are 100 percent solids and others are solution coatings. The formulator's recommendations should be followed in selecting the system for desired protection.

It is also desirable to follow the formulator's recommendations for the best application procedures, temperatures, and allowable working life. Generally, three coats must be applied to eliminate pinholes; glass flake to bridge the pinholes may also be used. Contact with epoxy resins or hardeners can cause skin irritation or allergic reactions, and proper protection is necessary.

Epoxy liners may be formed with reinforcement such as woven fabrics, mats, or chopped glass fiber. For example, on concrete that may undergo thermal movements, an isolation layer of two-component polysulfide joint sealant of the self-leveling type is troweled over the surface to form a 1/32-in.-thick layer of synthetic rubber. As soon as the rubber has cured, the epoxy coating is applied with a roller to a film thickness of 9 or 10 mils. Then fiber glass cloth is spread over the wet epoxy coating and pressed into it. A second epoxy coating is applied immediately to embed the fiber glass.

13. Neoprene: These coatings may be one- or two-part systems. The one-part system is used as a thinner film than the two-part and generally has a lower chemical resistance. It cures slowly at room temperature and some curing agents may limit its shelf life. The two-part system may require a holding period between mixing and application.

Application of either system should not begin for at least 10 days after removal of the forms to allow evaporation of water from the concrete. Some coatings require primers while others are designed to be self-priming. Adhesion is often improved by application of a diluted first coat to increase penetration of the surface. Each coat should be sufficiently solvent-dry before the next application; however, if it becomes too fully cured, it may swell and lose adhesion. Three coats of 2 to 3 mils each are normally recommended to eliminate the possibility of pinholes. For immersion service, minimum dry thickness should be 20 mils.

14. Polysulfide: These coatings may be one- or two-part systems. They do not harden with age and they remain rubbery over a broad temperature range. Thick coats of 20 to 25 mils can be applied at one time. For the one-part system, atmospheric moisture serves as the curing agent; when humidities are low, curing can be hastened by spraying with a fine water mist. The two-part system usually has a pot life of 30 to 45 minutes and becomes tack-free overnight.

15. Coal tar-epoxy: Coal tar-epoxy coatings are classified in three main types according to epoxy resin content: high-resin coatings for dry thicknesses of 15 mils; medium-resin coatings for integral linings of concrete pipe; and low-resin coatings for building nonsagging barriers up to 40 mils thick. The first type requires a special primer and its thickness is achieved in two coats. The other types do not require primers and may be applied in a single coat, but they require relatively long cure time. Some coal tar-epoxy resin coatings are catalytically cured—with a hardener, or with both hardener and catalyst.

Protective Treatments —Cont.

Coal tar-epoxy coatings are a two-package system. A combination of coal tar, filler, solvent, and epoxy resin may be in one package and the curing agent (commonly amines, polyamines, amine adducts, polyamides, or tertiary amines) in the other. These two packages are usually mixed in a ratio of 20:1 or 10:1, but the ratio may be lower. The coal tar, filler, solvent, and curing agent may also be blended together to make up one package and the epoxy resin kept separate for the other package. These two packages are generally mixed in a ratio of 3:1. The packages must be proportioned correctly to secure proper cure and chemical resistance. Storage life of the blends can vary from six months to two years, depending on formulation.

It is important that the two packages be thoroughly mixed, and power agitation is strongly recommended. Mixing small quantities is not recommended. Insufficient mixing will be revealed only after the coating has cured. For some coatings, a ½-hour waiting period between mixing and application is desired. Pot life is generally 3 to 4 hours at 70 deg. F., but it may vary from several minutes to 8 hours, depending on solvent content and formulation.

Coal tar-epoxy coatings should not be applied at temperatures below 50 deg. F. or when danger exists of their becoming wet within 24 hours of application. Spray applications generally result in better coverage. However, the sides of a short, stiff bristle brush or a long nap roller may be used. The second coat should be applied within 48 hours to prevent adhesion problems between coats. These coatings should not be put into service until a minimum of 5 days' curing time has been allowed.

16. Chemical-resistant masonry units and mortars: Three basic types of chemical-resistant masonry units are available: Type H brick, generally fire-clay; Type L brick, generally shale; and carbon and graphite brick, intended for use where additional chemical resistance is required. Types H and L brick should conform to Standard Specifications for Chemical-Resistant Masonry Units (ASTM C279).

Brick thickness generally varies from 1¼ to 3¾ in., depending upon severity of service. Brick surfaces should be scored or wire-cut (matt texture). The brick must, of course, be laid in mortar that is also resistant against the substance to which they are to be exposed.

The chemical resistance of mortars may be evaluated by Standard Method of Test for Chemical Resistance of Mortars (ASTM C267). The more commonly used chemical-resistant mortars *may also be used alone*, without masonry units, to form thick coatings–usually applied by trowel. These mortars are:

a. **Asphaltic and bituminous mortars**–supplied for use over a limited range of low temperatures. Some are sand-filled and some are not. They may be applied either as mastics that depend upon evaporation of solvent or as hot-melt compounds.

b. **Epoxy resin mortars**–two- or three-part systems with either amine or polyamide curing agents, they should conform to Standard Specifications for Chemical-Resistant Resin Mortars (ASTM C395). For their use, see the Recommended Practice for Use of Chemical-Resistant Resin Mortars (ASTM C399).

c. **Furan resin mortars**–should conform to ASTM C395. They require a primer to ensure satisfactory adhesion to concrete. For their use, see ASTM C399.

d. **Hydraulic cement mortars**–for their use, see the Recommended Practice for Use of Hydraulic Cement Mortars in Chemical-Resistant Masonry (ASTM C398).

e. **Phenolic resin mortars**–should conform to ASTM C395. For their use, see ASTM C399.

f. **Polyester resin mortars**–should conform to ASTM C395. They are limited in resistance to strong chemicals but will withstand mildly oxidizing solutions such as bleaches. For their use, see ASTM C399.

g. **Silicate mortars**–should conform to Standard Specifications for Chemically Setting Silicate and Silica Chemical-Resistant Mortars (ASTM C466). For their use, see the Recommended Practice for Use of

Protective Treatments—Cont.

Chemically Setting Chemical-Resistant Silicate and Silica Mortars (ASTM C397).

h. Sulfur mortars–should conform to Standard Specifications for Chemical-Resistant Sulfur Mortar (ASTM C287). For their use, see the Recommended Practice for Use of Chemical-Resistant Sulfur Mortars (ASTM C386).

A bed of mortar and an impervious membrane lining are usually placed between the masonry lining and concrete. Rubber and vinyl sheets or properly primed and hot-applied 3/8-in.-thick asphaltic materials, both plain and glass-cloth-reinforced, are preferred for the membrane lining, depending on the corrosive substance. The primer should conform to Standard Specifications for Primer for Use with Asphalt in Dampproofing and Waterproofing (ASTM D41), except that the asphalt content should be not less than 35 percent by weight. Floor slabs that are to receive a masonry lining should have a smooth wood-float finish. A slab having a steel-trowel finish may be too smooth for adhesion of the asphaltic membrane.

17. Sheet rubber: Soft natural and synthetic rubber sheets 1/8 to 1/2 in. thick may be cemented to concrete with special adhesives. Sometimes two layers of soft rubber are used as a base, with a single layer of hard rubber over them.

Chemical-resistant synthetics available as sheeting are neoprene, polyvinylidene chloride-acrylonitrile, plasticized polyvinyl chloride, polyisobutylene, butyl, nitrile, polysulfide, and chlorosulfonated polyethylene rubbers.

18. Resin sheets: Synthetic resins, particularly polyester, epoxy, and polyvinyl chloride, are available as sheet materials. *These sheets are not referred to in the tables but may be used wherever comparable resin coatings are recommended.* Frequently glass-fiber-reinforced, they may be cemented to concrete with special adhesives.

19. Lead sheet: In the United States, lead sheet used for chemical resistance is called "chemical lead." The sheets should be as large as possible (to minimize the number of joints) but not too heavy to handle–up to 8x20 ft. for the thinnest. Thicknesses range from 1/64 to 1/2 in. Lead may be cemented to concrete with an asphaltic paint. Each sheet should be overlapped and the seam welded by conventional lead-burning techniques. If the lead is to be subjected to high temperatures, it may be covered with chemical-resistant masonry to reduce thermal stresses.

20. Glass: Two types have been used for corrosion resistance: high-silica glass and borosilicate glass. Borosilicate glass, the more alkali-resistant material, is recommended because alkalies in concrete may cause glass etching. Glass may be cemented to the concrete. Thermal shock is often a cause of failure in glass-lined structures.

ACIDS

Material	Effect on concrete	Protective treatments
Acetic:		
<10%	Slow disintegration	1, 2, 9, 10, 12, 14, 16 (b, c, e, f, g, h)
30%	Slow disintegration	9, 10, 14, 16 (c, e, f, g)
100% (glacial)	Slow disintegration	9, 16 (e, g)
Acid waters (pH of 6.5 or less)	Slow disintegration.* Natural acid waters may erode surface mortar but then action usually stops	1, 2, 3, 6, 8, 9, 10, 11, 12, 13, 16 (b, c, e, f, g, h), 17
Arsenious	None	
Boric	Negligible effect	2, 6, 7, 8, 9, 10, 12, 13, 15, 16 (b, c, e, f, g, h), 17, 19
Butyric	Slow disintegration	3, 4, 8, 9, 10, 12, 16 (b, c, e, f)
Carbolic	Slow disintegration	1, 2, 16 (c, e, g), 17
Carbonic (soda water)	0.9 to 3 ppm of carbon dioxide dissolved in natural waters disintegrates concrete slowly	2, 3, 4, 8, 9, 10, 12, 13, 15, 16 (b, c, e, f, h), 17
Chromic:		
5%	None*	2, 6, 7, 8, 9, 10, 16 (f, g, h), 19
50%	None*	16 (g), 19
Formic:		
10%	Slow disintegration	2, 5, 6, 7, 12, 13, 16 (b, c, e, g), 17
90%	Slow disintegration	2, 7, 13, 16 (c, e, g), 17
Humic	Slow disintegration possible, depending on humus material	1, 2, 3, 9, 12, 15, 16 (b, c, e)
Hydrochloric:		
10%	Rapid disintegration, including steel	2, 5, 6, 7, 8, 9, 10, 12, 14, 16 (b, c, e, f, g, h), 17, 19, 20
37%	Rapid disintegration, including steel	5, 6, 8, 9, 10, 16 (c, e, f, g, h)
Hydrofluoric:		
10%	Rapid disintegration, including steel	5, 6, 7, 8, 9, 12, 16 (carbon and graphite brick; b, c, e, h), 17
75%	Rapid disintegration, including steel	16 (carbon and graphite brick; e, h), 17
Hypochlorous, 10%	Slow disintegration	5, 8, 9, 10, 16 (f, g)
Lactic, 5%	Slow disintegration	3, 4, 5, 7, 8, 9, 10, 11, 12, 13, 15, 16 (b, c, e, f, g, h), 17
Nitric:		
2%	Rapid disintegration	6, 8, 9, 10, 13, 16 (f, g, h), 20
40%	Rapid disintegration	8, 16 (g)
Oleic, 100%	None	
Oxalic	No disintegration. It protects concrete against acetic acid, carbon dioxide, and salt water. POISONOUS, it must not be used on concrete in contact with food or drinking water.	
Perchloric, 10%	Disintegration	8, 10, 16 (e, f, g, h)
Phosphoric:		
10%	Slow disintegration	1, 2, 3, 5, 6, 7, 8, 9, 10, 11, 12, 13, 14, 15, 16 (b, c, e, f, g, h), 17, 19
85%	Slow disintegration	1, 2, 3, 5, 7, 8, 9, 10, 13, 14, 15, 16 (c, e, f, g, h), 17, 19
Stearic	Rapid disintegration	5, 6, 8, 9, 10, 11, 12, 13, 15, 16 (b, c, e, f, g, h), 17
Sulfuric:		
10%	Rapid disintegration	5, 6, 7, 8, 9, 10, 12, 13, 14, 15, 16 (b, c, e, f, g, h), 17, 19, 20
110% (oleum)	Disintegration	16 (g), 19
Sulfurous	Rapid disintegration	6, 7, 9, 11, 12, 13, 16 (b, c, e, h), 19, 20
Tannic	Slow disintegration	1, 2, 3, 6, 7, 8, 9, 11, 12, 13, 16 (b, c, e, g), 17
Tartaric, solution	None. See wine under "Miscellaneous."	

*In porous or cracked concrete, it attacks steel. Steel corrosion may cause concrete to spall.

SALTS AND ALKALIES (SOLUTIONS)*

Material	Effect on concrete	Protective treatments
Bicarbonate: Ammonium Sodium	None	

*Dry materials generally have no effect.

Salts and Alkalies (Solutions)—Cont.

Substance	Effect	References
Bisulfate: Ammonium**, Sodium	Disintegration	5, 6, 7, 8, 9, 10, 11, 12, 13, 14, 15, 16 (b, c, e, f, h), 17
Bisulfite: Sodium	Disintegration	5, 6, 7, 8, 9, 10, 12, 13, 16 (b, c, e, f, h), 17
Calcium (sulfite solution)	Rapid disintegration	7, 8, 9, 10, 12, 13, 16 (b, c, e, f, h), 17
Bromide, sodium	Slow disintegration	1, 2, 5, 6, 7, 8, 9, 10, 11, 12, 13, 14, 16 (b, c, e, f, h), 17
Carbonate: Ammonium, Potassium, Sodium	None	
Chlorate, sodium	Slow disintegration	1, 4, 6, 7, 8, 9, 10, 16 (f, g, h), 17, 19
Chloride: Calcium†, Potassium†, Sodium†, Strontium	None, unless concrete is alternately wet and dry with the solution**	1, 3, 4, 5, 6, 7, 8, 9, 10, 11, 12, 13, 15, 16 (b, c, e, f, g, h), 17
Ammonium, Copper, Ferric (iron), Ferrous, Magnesium, Mercuric, Mercurous, Zinc	Slow disintegration**	1, 3, 4, 5, 6, 7, 8, 9, 10, 11, 12, 13, 15, 16 (b, c, e, f, g, h), 17
Aluminum	Rapid disintegration**	1, 3, 4, 5, 6, 7, 8, 9, 10, 11, 12, 13, 15, 16 (b, c, e, f, h), 17
Chromate, sodium	None	
Cyanide: Ammonium, Potassium, Sodium	Slow disintegration	7, 8, 9, 12, 13, 16 (b, c), 17
Dichromate: Sodium	Slow disintegration with dilute solutions	1, 2, 6, 7, 8, 9, 10, 11, 12, 13, 15, 16 (b, c, e, f, h), 17
Potassium	Disintegration	1, 2, 6, 7, 8, 9, 10, 11, 12, 13, 15, 16 (b, c, e, f, h), 17
Ferrocyanide, sodium	None	
Fluoride: Ammonium, Sodium	Slow disintegration	3, 4, 8, 9, 13, 16 (a, c, e, h), 17
Fluosilicate, magnesium	None	
Hexametaphosphate, sodium	Slow disintegration	5, 6, 7, 8, 9, 12, 13, 15, 16 (b, c, e), 17
Hydroxide: Ammonium, Barium, Calcium, Potassium 15%††, Sodium 10%††	None	
Potassium, 25%; Sodium, 20%	Disintegration. Use of calcareous aggregate lessens attack.	5, 7, 8, 12, 13, 14, 15, 16 (carbon and graphite brick; b, c) 17
Nitrate: Calcium, Ferric, Zinc	None	
Lead, Magnesium, Potassium, Sodium	Slow disintegration	2, 5, 6, 7, 8, 9, 10, 11, 12, 13, 16 (b, c, e, f, g, h), 17, 20
Ammonium	Disintegration**	2, 5, 6, 8, 9, 10, 11, 12, 13, 16 (b, c, e, f, g, h), 17, 20
Nitrite, sodium	Slow disintegration	1, 2, 5, 6, 7, 8, 9, 12, 13, 16 (b, c), 17
Orthophosphate, sodium (dibasic and tribasic)	None	
Oxalate, ammonium	None	
Perborate, sodium	Slow disintegration	1, 4, 7, 8, 9, 10, 13, 16 (d, f, g, h), 17

**In porous or cracked concrete, it attacks steel. Steel corrosion may cause concrete to spall.

†Frequently used as a de-icer for concrete pavements. If the concrete contains insufficient entrained air or has not been air-dried for at least 30 days after completion of curing, repeated application may cause surface scaling. See de-icers under "Miscellaneous."

††If concrete is made with reactive aggregates, disruptive expansions may occur.

Salts and Alkalies (Solutions) - Cont.

Material	Effect on concrete	Protective treatments
Perchlorate, sodium	Slow disintegration	6, 7, 8, 10, 16 (f, g, h), 17
Permanganate, potassium	None	1, 2, 5, 7, 8, 9, 10, 12, 13, 16 (b, c, e, f, h), 17
Persulfate, potassium	Disintegration of concrete with inadequate sulfate resistance	5, 6, 7, 8, 9, 12, 15, 16 (b, c), 17
Phosphate, sodium (mono-basic)	Slow disintegration	
Pyrophosphate, sodium	None	
Stannate, sodium	None	
Sulfate: Ammonium	Disintegration**	5, 6, 7, 8, 9, 10, 11, 12, 13, 14, 15, 16 (b, c, e, f, g, h), 17
Aluminum Calcium Cobalt Copper Ferric Ferrous (iron vitriol) Magnesium (epsom salt) Manganese Nickel Potassium	Disintegration of concrete with inadequate sulfate resistance. Concrete products cured in high-pressure steam are highly resistant to sulfates.	1, 3, 4, 5, 6, 7, 8, 9, 10, 11, 12, 13, 15, 16 (b, c, e, f, g, h), 17
Potassium aluminum (alum) Sodium Zinc	Disintegration of concrete with inadequate sulfate resistance. Concrete products cured in high-pressure steam are highly resistant to sulfates.	1, 3, 4, 5, 6, 7, 8, 9, 10, 11, 12, 13, 15, 16 (b, c, e, f, g, h), 17
Sulfide: Copper Ferric Potassium	None unless sulfates are present	7, 8, 9, 10, 12, 13, 15, 16 (b, c, e, f, h), 17
Sodium	Slow disintegration	6, 7, 8, 9, 11, 12, 13, 15, 16 (b, c), 17
Ammonium	Disintegration	7, 8, 9, 12, 13, 15, 16 (a, b, c, e), 17
Sulfite: Sodium	None unless sulfates are present	1, 2, 5, 6, 7, 8, 9, 11, 12, 13, 15, 16 (b, c, e), 17
Ammonium	Disintegration	8, 9, 12, 15, 16 (b, c, e, h), 17
Superphosphate, ammonium	Disintegration**	8, 9, 12, 13, 15, 16 (b, c, e), 17, 19
Tetraborate, sodium (borax)	Slow disintegration	5, 6, 7, 8, 9, 10, 11, 12, 13, 15, 16 (b, c, e, f, g, h), 17
Thiosulfate: Sodium	Slow disintegration of concrete with inadequate sulfate resistance	1, 2, 5, 6, 7, 8, 9, 10, 12, 13, 15, 16 (b, c, e), 17
Ammonium	Disintegration	8, 9, 12, 13, 15, 16 (b, c, e), 17

PETROLEUM OILS

Material	Effect on concrete	Protective treatments
Heavy oil below 35° Baumé* Paraffin	None	
Gasoline Kerosene Light oil above 35° Baumé* Ligroin Lubricating oil* Machine oil* Mineral spirits	None. Impervious concrete is required to prevent loss from penetration, and surface treatments are generally used.	1, 2, 3, 8, 10, 11, 12, 14, 16 (b, c, e, f), 17, 19
Gasoline, high octane	None. Surface treatments are generally used to prevent contamination with alkalies in concrete.	11, 14, 17

*May contain some vegetable or fatty oils and the concrete should be protected from such oils.

COAL TAR DISTILLATES

Material	Effect on concrete	Protective treatments
Alizarin Anthracene Carbazole Chrysen Pitch	None	

Coal Tar Distillates -Cont.

	Effect on concrete	Protective treatments
Benzol (benzene), Cumol (cumene), Phenanthrene, Toluol (toluene), Xylol (xylene)	None. Impervious concrete is required to prevent loss from penetration, and surface treatments are generally used.	1, 2, 10, 11, 12, 16 (b, c, e, f, g), 19
Creosote, Cresol, Dinitrophenol, Phenol, 5 to 25%	Slow disintegration	1, 2, 16 (c, e, g), 17, 19
Ethylene glycol**	Slow disintegration	1, 2, 7, 10, 12, 13, 14, 16 (b, c, e, f, g, h), 17

*Impervious concrete is required to prevent loss from penetration, and surface treatments are generally used.

**Frequently used as de-icer for airplanes. Heavy spillage on concrete containing insufficient entrained air may cause surface scaling.

VEGETABLE OILS

Material	Effect on concrete	Protective treatments
Rosin and rosin oil	None	
Turpentine	Mild attack and considerable penetration	1, 2, 11, 12, 14, 16 (b, c, e)
Almond, China wood*, Linseed*, Olive, Peanut, Poppy seed, Soybean*, Tung*, Walnut	Slow disintegration	1, 2, 8, 10, 11, 12, 14, 16 (b, c, e, f), 17. For expensive cooking oils, use 20.
Margarine	Slow disintegration—faster with melted margarine	1, 2, 8, 10, 11, 12, 13, 16 (b, c, e, f)
Castor, Cocoa bean, Cocoa butter, Coconut, Cottonseed, Mustard, Rapeseed	Disintegration, especially if exposed to air	1, 2, 8, 10, 11, 12, 14, 16 (b, c, e, f), 17

*Applied in thin coats, the material quickly oxidizes and has no effect. The effect indicated above is for constant exposure to the material in liquid form.

SOLVENTS AND ALCOHOLS

Material	Effect on concrete	Protective treatments
Carbon tetrachloride	None*	1, 2, 10, 12, 16 (b, c, e, g)
Ethyl alcohol	None* (see de-icers under "Miscellaneous")	1, 2, 5, 7, 10, 12, 13, 14, 16 (b, c, e, f, g, h), 17, 19
Ethyl ether	None*	11, 12, 16 (c, e), 19
Methyl alcohol	None*	1, 2, 5, 7, 10, 12, 13, 14, 16 (b, c, e, f, g, h), 17, 19
Methyl ethyl ketone	None*	16 (c, e), 17, 19
Methyl isoamyl ketone	None*	16 (c, e), 17
Methyl isobutyl	None*	16 (c, e), 17
Perchloroethylene	None*	12, 16 (b, c, e)
t-Butyl alcohol	None*	1, 2, 5, 7, 10, 12, 13, 14, 16 (b, c, e, f, g, h), 17, 19
Trichloroethylene	None*	1, 2, 12, 16 (b, c, e, g)
Acetone	None.* However, acetone may contain acetic acid as impurity (see under "Acids").	1, 2, 10, 16 (c, e, g), 17, 19
Carbon disulfide	Slow disintegration possible	1, 2, 11, 16 (c, e, g)
Glycerin (glycerol)	Slow disintegration possible	1, 2, 3, 4, 7, 11, 12, 13, 16 (b, c, e, f, g), 17

FATS AND FATTY ACIDS (ANIMAL)

Material	Effect on concrete	Protective treatments
Fish liquor	Disintegration	3, 8, 10, 12, 13, 16 (b, c, e, f), 17

84

Fats and Fatty Acids (Animal) – Cont.

Fish oil	Slow disintegration with most fish oils	1, 2, 3, 8, 10, 12, 13, 16 (b, c, e, f), 17
Whale oil	Slow disintegration	1, 2, 3, 8, 10, 12, 13, 16 (b, c, e, f), 17
Neatsfoot oil Tallow and tallow oil	Slow disintegration	1, 2, 3, 8, 10, 12, 13, 16 (b, c, e, f), 17
Beef fat Horse fat Lamb fat	Slow disintegration with solid fat—faster with melted	1, 2, 3, 8, 10, 12, 13, 16 (b, c, e, f), 17
Lard and lard oil	Slow disintegration—faster with oil	1, 2, 3, 8, 10, 12, 13, 16 (b, c, e, f), 17
Slaughterhouse wastes	Disintegration due to organic acids	8, 12, 13, 16 (b, c, e)

MISCELLANEOUS

Material	Effect on concrete	Protective treatments
Alum	See sulfate, potassium aluminum, under "Salts and Alkalies"	
Ammonia: Liquid	None, unless it contains harmful ammonium salts (see under "Salts and Alkalies")	
Vapors	Possible slow disintegration of moist concrete and steel attacked in porous or cracked moist concrete	8, 9, 10, 12, 13, 16 (a, b, c, f), 17
Ashes: Cold	Harmful if wet, when sulfides and sulfates leach out (see sulfate, sodium, under "Salts and Alkalies")	1, 2, 3, 8, 9, 12, 13, 16 (b, c, e)
Hot	Thermal expansion	16 (calcium aluminate cement, fireclay, and refractory-silicate-clay mortars)
Automobile and diesel exhaust gases	Possible disintegration of moist concrete by action of carbonic, nitric, or sulfurous acid (see under "Acids")	1, 5, 8, 12, 16 (b, c, e)
Baking soda	None	8, 10, 11, 12, 16 (b, c, f), 17, coatings made and applied by Borsari Tank Corp. of America, 605 Third Ave., New York, N.Y. 10016
Beer	No progressive disintegration, but in beer storage and fermenting tanks a special coating is used to guard against beer contamination. Beer may contain, as fermentation products, acetic, carbonic, lactic, or tannic acids (see under "Acids").	
Bleaching solution	See the specific chemical, such as hypochlorous acid, sodium hypochlorite, sulfurous acid, etc.	
Borax (salt)	See tetraborate, sodium, under "Salts and Alkalies"	
Brine	See chloride, sodium, or other salts under "Salts and Alkalies"	
Bromine	Disintegration if bromine gaseous—or if a liquid containing hydrobromic acid and moisture	10, 13, 16 (f, g)
Buttermilk	Slow disintegration due to lactic acid	2, 3, 4, 7, 8, 9, 10, 11, 12, 13, 16 (b, c, e, f), 17
Butyl stearate	Slow disintegration	8, 9, 10, 16 (b, c, e)
Carbon dioxide	Gas may cause permanent shrinkage. See carbonic acid under "Acids."	1, 2, 3, 6, 8, 9, 10, 11, 12, 13, 15, 16 (b, c, e, f, h), 17
Caustic soda	See hydroxide, sodium, under "Salts and Alkalies"	
Chile saltpeter	See nitrate, sodium, under "Salts and Alkalies"	
Chlorine gas	Slow disintegration of moist concrete	2, 8, 9, 10, 16 (f, g), 17
Chrome plating solutions	Slow disintegration	7, 8, 9, 10, 16 (f, g), 20
Cider	Slow disintegration. See acetic acid under "Acids."	1, 2, 9, 10, 12, 14, 16 (b, c, e, f, g), 17
Cinders cold and hot	See ashes	
Coal	None, unless coal is high in pyrites (sulfide of iron) and moisture. Sulfides leaching from damp coal may oxidize to sulfurous or sulfuric acid, or ferrous sulfate (see under "Acids" and "Salts and Alkalies"). Rate is greatly retarded by deposit of an insoluble film.	1, 2, 3, 6, 7, 8, 9, 12, 13, 16 (b, c, e, h), 17

Miscellaneous –Cont.

Material	Effect	References
Coke	Sulfides leaching from damp coke may oxidize to sulfurous or sulfuric acid (see under "Acids").	1, 2, 3, 6, 7, 8, 9, 12, 13, 16 (b, c, e, h)
Copper plating solutions	None	
Corn syrup (glucose)	Slow disintegration	1, 2, 3, 7, 8, 9, 12, 13, 16 (b, c, e), 17
De-icers	Chlorides (calcium and sodium), urea, and ethyl alcohol cause scaling of non-air-entrained concrete.	50% solution of boiled linseed oil in kerosene, soybean oil, modified castor oil, cottonseed oil, sand-filled epoxy, or coal-tar epoxy
Distiller's slop	Slow disintegration due to lactic acid	1, 8, 9, 10, 12, 13, 15, 16 (b, c, e, f, h), 17
Fermenting fruits, grains, vegetables, or extracts	Slow disintegration. Industrial fermentation processes produce lactic acid (see under "Acids").	1, 2, 3, 8, 9, 12, 16 (b, c, e), 17
Flue gases	Hot gases (400-1100° F.) cause thermal stresses. Cooled, condensed sulfurous, hydrochloric acids disintegrate concrete slowly.	9 (high melting), 16 (g, fireclay mortar)
Formaldehyde, 37% (formalin)	Slow disintegration due to formic acid formed in solution	2, 5, 6, 8, 10, 11, 12, 13, 14, 16 (b, c, e, f, g, h), 17, 20
Fruit juices	Little if any effect for most fruit juices as tartaric and citric acids do not appreciably affect concrete. Sugar and hydrofluoric and other acids cause disintegration.	1, 2, 3, 6, 7, 8, 9, 11, 12, 16 (b, c, e), 17
Gas water	Ammonium salts seldom present in sufficient quantity to disintegrate concrete	9, 12, 16 (b, c)
Glyceryl tristearate	None	
Honey	None	
Hydrogen sulfide	Slow disintegration in moist oxidizing environments where hydrogen sulfide converts to sulfurous acid	1, 2, 5, 6, 7, 8, 9, 10, 11, 12, 13, 16 (b, c, e, f, g, h), 17, 19
Iodine	Slow disintegration	1, 2, 6, 12, 13, 16 (b, c, e, g), 17
Lead refining solution	Slow disintegration	1, 2, 6, 8, 9, 12, 16 (carbon and graphite brick; b, c, e, h), 17, 20
Lignite oils	Slow disintegration if fatty oils present	1, 2, 6, 8, 10, 12, 16 (b, c, e, f)
Lye	See hydroxide, sodium and potassium, under "Salts and Alkalies"	
Manure	Slow disintegration	1, 2, 8, 9, 12, 13, 16 (b, c, e)
Mash, fermenting	Slow disintegration due to acetic and lactic acids and sugar	1, 8, 9, 10, 12, 13, 16 (b, c)
Milk	None, unless milk is sour. Then lactic acid disintegrates concrete slowly.	3, 4, 8, 9, 10, 11, 12, 13, 16 (b, c, f), 17
Mine water, waste	Sulfides, sulfates, or acids present disintegrate concrete and attack steel in porous or cracked concrete	1, 2, 5, 8, 9, 10, 12, 13, 15, 16 (b, c, e, f, h), 17
Molasses	Slow disintegration at temperatures $\geq 120°$ F.	1, 2, 7, 8, 9, 12, 13,¹ 16 (b, c, e), 17
Nickel plating solutions	Slow disintegration due to nickel ammonium sulfate	2, 5, 6, 7, 8, 9, 10, 13, 16 (c, e, f), 17
Niter	See nitrate, potassium, under "Salts and Alkalies"	
Ores	Sulfides leaching from damp ores may oxidize to sulfuric acid or ferrous sulfate (see under "Acids" and "Salts and Alkalies")	2, 9, 10, 12, 13, 15, 16 (b, c, e, f, g), 17
Pickling brine	Steel attacked in porous or cracked concrete. See salts, boric acid, or sugar.	1, 7, 8, 9, 12, 13, 16 (b, c, e, h), 17
Sal ammoniac	See chloride, ammonium, under "Salts and Alkalies"	
Sal soda	See carbonate, sodium, under "Salts and Alkalies"	
Saltpeter	See nitrate, potassium, under "Salts and Alkalies"	
Sauerkraut	Slow disintegration possible due to lactic acid. Flavor impaired by concrete.	
Sea water	Disintegration of concrete with inadequate sulfate resistance and steel attacked in porous or cracked concrete	1, 2, 8, 9, 10, 12, 13, 16 (b, c, e, f), 17

Miscellaneous -Cont.

Substance	Effect	References
Sewage and sludge	Usually not harmful. See hydrogen sulfide	
Silage	Slow disintegration due to acetic, butyric, and lactic acids, and sometimes fermenting agents of hydrochloric or sulfuric acids	3, 4, 8, 9, 10, 12, 16 (b, c, e, f)
Sodium hypochlorite	Slow disintegration	7, 8, 9, 10, 13, 16 (d, f), 17
Sugar (sucrose)	None with dry sugar on thoroughly cured concrete. Sugar solutions may disintegrate concrete slowly.	1, 2, 3, 7, 8, 9, 10, 12, 13, 15, 16 (b, c, e, f), 17
Sulfite liquor	Disintegration	1, 2, 3, 5, 6, 8, 9, 10, 12, 13, 16 (b, c, e, f, h), 17, 19
Sulfur dioxide	None if dry. With moisture, sulfur dioxide forms sulfurous acid.	2, 5, 6, 8, 9, 10, 12, 13, 16 (b, c, e, f, g, h), 17, 19
Tanning bark	Slow disintegration possible if damp. See tanning liquor below.	1, 2, 3, 6, 8, 9, 11, 12, 13, 16 (b, c, e), 17
Tanning liquor	None with most liquors, including chromium. If liquor is acid, it disintegrates concrete.	1, 2, 3, 5, 6, 8, 9, 11, 12, 13, 16 (b, c, e), 17
Tobacco	Slow disintegration if organic acids present	1, 8, 9, 10, 12, 13, 16 (b, c, e, f), 17

Substance	Effect	References
Trisodium phosphate	None	
Urea	None (see de-icers)	
Urine	None, but steel attacked in porous or cracked concrete	7, 8, 12, 13, 16 (b, c, e)
Vinegar	Slow disintegration due to acetic acid	9, 12, 16 (b, c, e, h), 17
Washing soda	None	
Water, soft (<75 ppm of carbonate hardness)	Leaching of hydrated lime by flowing water in porous or cracked concrete	2, 3, 4, 8, 9, 10, 12, 13, 16 (b, c, e, f, h), 17
Whey	Slow disintegration due to lactic acid	3, 4, 5, 7, 8, 9, 10, 12, 13, 16 (b, c, e, f, h), 17
Wine	None—but taste of first wine batch may be affected unless concrete has been given tartaric acid treatment	For fine wines, 2 or 3 applications of tartaric acid solution (1 lb. tartaric acid in 3 pints water), 2, 8, 12, 16 (b), 20
Wood pulp	None	
Zinc refining solutions	Disintegration if hydrochloric or sulfuric acids present	8, 9, 10, 12, 13, 16 (b, c, e, f, h), 17
Zinc slag	Zinc sulfate (see under "Salts and Alkalies") may be formed by oxidation	8, 9, 10, 12, 13, 16 (b, c, e, f, h), 17

KEY WORDS: acid resistance, acids, alkalies, bitumens, carbonate rocks, chemical attack, chemical tests, coatings, concrete durability, concrete, corrosion, curing compounds, linings, masonry, mix proportioning, mortar linings, mortars (material), oils, paints, parting agents, plastics, polymers, protective coatings, resin cements, rubber, surface defects, surface treatments, synthetic resins, thermoplastic resins, thermosetting resins.

ABSTRACT: Design considerations to increase resistance of concrete to aggressive chemical exposures for substantial periods of time are discussed. Surface preparation and the more common protective treatments are described. Tables are included as a guide for determining when to consider various treatments for chemical resistance.

REFERENCE: *Effect of Various Substances on Concrete and Protective Treatments, Where Required* (IS001.03T), Portland Cement Association, 1968.

MANUFACTURERS OF TREATMENTS TO PROTECT CONCRETE
AGAINST AGGRESSIVE SUBSTANCES--DECEMBER 1968*

1. Magnesium and Zinc Fluosilicates

American Agricultural Chemical Co., 50 Church St., New York, N.Y. 10007
American Cyanamid Co., Industrial Chemical Div., 30 Rockefeller Plaza, New York, N.Y. 10020
American Fluoride Corp., 855 Avenue of the Americas, New York, N.Y. 10001
Berkshire Chemicals, Inc., 155 E. 44th St., New York, N.Y. 10014
Davison Chemical Div., W. R. Grace & Co., 101 N. Charles St., Baltimore, Md. 21201
Devoe/Truscon, Div. of Celanese Coatings Co., Box 1863, Louisville, Ky. 40201
Dewey & Almy Chemical Div., W. R. Grace & Co., 62 Whittemore Ave., Cambridge, Mass. 02140
E. I. DuPont de Nemours & Co., Inc., Wilmington, Del.
Harshaw Chemical Co., 1933 E. 97th St., Cleveland, Ohio 44106
Hummel Chemical Co., Inc., 185 Foundry, Newark, N.J. 07105
Sika Chemical Corp., 35 Gregory Ave., Passaic, N.J. 07055
Sonneborn Building Products, Inc., Div. of DeSoto Chemical Coatings, Inc., 1700 S. Mt. Prospect Road, Des Plaines, Ill. 60018
G. H. Tennant Co., 761 N. Lilac Drive, Minneapolis, Minn. 55422
Toch Bros., Inc., 250 Vreeland Ave., Patterson, N.J. 07504

*This list is furnished to assist in locating manufacturers and does not imply Portland Cement Association endorsement of any of their products.

88

Manufacturers of Treatments -Cont.

2. Sodium Silicate

Allied Chemical Corp., General Chemical Div., Morristown, N.J. 07960

American Cyanamid Co., Industrial Chemicals Div., Berdan Ave., Wayne, N.J. 07470

Big Ben Chemicals & Solvents, Inc., 626 S. Michigan Ave., Chicago, Ill. 60605

Chemical Products Corp., 48 Atlanta Road, Cartersville, Ga. 30120

Diamond Alkali Co., 300 Union Commerce Bldg., Cleveland, Ohio 44115

E. I. DuPont de Nemours & Co., Inc., Industrial & Biochemicals Dept., Wilmington, Del.

Globe Chemical Co., Inc., 25 Murray Road & Big Four RR, Cincinnati, Ohio 45217

Philadelphia Quartz Co., 1123 Public Ledger Bldg., Philadelphia, Pa. 19106

Philipp Brothers Chemicals, Inc., 10-12 Columbus Circle, New York, N.Y. 10023

3. Drying Oils (Linseed)

Commercially available locally

4. Coumarone-Indene*

Allied Chemical Corp., Barrett Div., 40 Rector St., New York, N.Y. 10006

Alabama Binder & Chemical Corp., Tuscaloosa, Ala.

Crowley Tar Products Co., Inc., 269 Madison Ave., New York, N.Y. 10010

Pennsylvania Industrial Chemical Corp., 127 State St., Clairton, Pa. 15025

Neville Chemical Co., 1938 Neville Island, Pittsburgh, Pa. 15225

---

*Basic material manufacturers are listed instead of formulators.

Manufacturers of Treatments - Cont.

5. Styrene-Butadiene*

Goodyear Tire & Rubber Co., Chemical Div., 1144 E. Market St., Akron, Ohio 44316

Marbon Chemical Co., Div. of Borg-Warner Co., P.O. Box 68, Washington, W.Va. 26181

6. Chlorinated Rubber*

Hercules, Inc., 910 Market St., Wilmington, Del. 19801

Chemical Manufacturing Co., Inc., Sub. of Imperial Chemical Industries Ltd., 444 Madison Ave., New York, N.Y. 10022

7. Chlorosulfonated Polyethylene (Hypalon)*

E. I. DuPont-de Nemours & Co., Inc., Elastomers Dept., Wilmington, Del. 19801

8. Vinyls

Allied Chemical Corp., Solvay Process Div., 40 Rector St., New York, N.Y. 10006

Amercoat Corp., 201 N. Berry St., Brea, Calif. 92621

Atlas Minerals and Chemicals Div., The Electric Storage Battery Co., 121 Norman St., Mertztown, Pa. 19539

The Electric Storage Battery Co., 121 Norman St., Mertztown, Pa. 15939

Borden Chemical Co., 511 Lancaster St., Leominster, Mass. 01453

Carboline Co., 328-R Hanley Industrial Court, St. Louis, Mo. 63144

Ceilcote Co., 140 Sheldon Road, Berea, Ohio 44017

Celanese Corp., 522 Fifth Ave., New York, N.Y. 10036

Diamond Alkali Co., 300 Union Commerce Bldg., Cleveland, Ohio 44115

Dow Chemical Co., Abbott Road, Midland, Mich. 48640

90

Manufacturers of Treatments - Cont.

E. I. DuPont de Nemours & Co., Inc., Plastic Dept., DuPont Bldg., Wilmington, Del. 19801

Essex Chemical Corp., BFC Div., 1401 Broad St., Clinton, N.J. 08809

Ethyl Corp., 100 Park Ave., New York, N.Y. 10017

Gates Engineering Div., Glidden Co., 58 Kern Ave., Wilmington, Del. 19899

B. F. Goodrich Chemical Co., 3135-T Euclid Ave., Cleveland, Ohio 44115

Goodyear Tire & Rubber Co., Inc., Chemical Div., 1144 E. Market St., Akron, Ohio 44316

Jones-Dabney Co., Resins & Chemicals Div., Louisville, Ky. 40208

Pittsburgh Plate Glass Co., Coatings & Resins Div., One Gateway Center, Pittsburgh, Pa. 15222

Plas-Chem Corp., 6177 Maple St., St. Louis, Mo. 63130

Reichhold Chemicals Inc., 525 N. Broadway, White Plains, N.Y. 10603

Stauffer Chemical Co., Plastics Div., 380 Madison Ave., New York, N.Y. 10017

Union Carbide Corp., Plastics Div., 270 Park Ave., New York, N.Y. 10017

U.S. Stoneware Co., 5300 E. Tallmadge Ave., Akron, Ohio 44309

9. Bituminous Paints, Mastics, and Enamels

Allied Chemical Corp., Barrett Div., 40 Rector St., New York, N.Y. 10006

Amercoat Corp., 201 N. Berry St., Brea, Calif. 92621

Atlas Minerals and Chemicals Div., The Electric Storage Battery Co., 121 Norman St., Mertztown, Pa. 19539

Barber Asphalt Paving Co., Barber, N.J.

W. A. Briggs Bitumen Co., 3303 Richmond St., Philadelphia, Pa. 19134

Buckeye Paint & Varnish Co., 199 S. St. Clair St., Toledo, Ohio 43602

Ceilcote Co., 140 Sheldon Road, Berea, Ohio 44017

Certain-teed Products Corp., 120 E. Lancaster Ave., Ardmore, Pa. 19003

Devoe-Truscon, Div. of Celanese Coatings Co., Box 1863, Louisville, Ky. 40201

Dewey & Almy Chemical Div., W. R. Grace & Co., 62 Whittemore Ave., Cambridge, Mass. 02140

Manufacturers of Treatments — Cont.

Flintkote Co., 30 Rockefeller Plaza, New York, N.Y. 10020

Glidden Co., General Paint Div., 1002 - 16th St., San Francisco, Calif. 94107

Inertol Co., Sub. of Koppers Co., 480 Frelinghuysen Ave., Newark, N.J. 07114

Johns-Manville, 22 E. 40th St., New York, N.Y. 10016

Koppers Co., Inc., Tar & Chemical Div., Koppers Bldg., Pittsburgh, Pa. 15219

Maintenance, Inc. Wooster, Ohio 44691

Plas-Chem Corp., 6177 Maple St., St. Louis, Mo. 63130

Reilly Tar & Chemical Corp., 11 S. Meridian St., Indianapolis, Ind. 46204

Reliance Paint Co., 64 S. 6th St., Brooklyn, N.Y. 11215

Ruberoid Co., 733 Third Ave., New York, N.Y. 10017

Rulon Co., Div. of Colonial Industries, Inc., Linwood & Pine Aves., Maple Shade, N.J. 08052

Sika Chemical Corp., 35 Gregory Ave., Passaic, N.J. 07055

L. Sonneborn Sons, Inc., 298 Park Ave., South, New York, N.Y. 10017

Stonhard Co., One Park Ave., Maple Shade, N.J. 08052

Toch Bros., Inc. 250 Vreeland Ave., Paterson, N.J. 07504

Tropical Paint Co., 1210-1250 W. 70th St., Cleveland, Ohio 44102

Vita-Var Co., Div. of Textron Industries, Inc., 177 Oakwood Ave., Orange, N.J. 07050

Witco Chemical Co., 277 Park Ave., New York, N.Y. 10017

10. Polyester

Allied Chemical Corp., Barrett Div., 42 Rector St., New York, N.Y. 10016

American Cyanamid Co., Plastics & Resins Div., Wallingford, Conn. 06492

Archer Daniels Midland Co., 733 Marquette Ave., Minneapolis, Minn. 55440

Atlas Chemical Industries, Inc., New Murphy Road, Wilmington, Del.

Ceilcote Co., 140 Sheldon Road, Berea, Ohio 44017

Celanese Corp., Plastics Div., 744 Broad St., Newark, N.J. 07102

Chevron Chemical Co., Oronite Div., 200 Bush St., San Francisco, Calif. 94104

Cook Paint & Varnish Co., 1412 Knox, North Kansas City, Mo. 64116

DeSoto Chemical Coatings, Inc., 1800 S. Mt. Prospect Road, Des Plaines, Ill. 60018

Manufacturers of Treatments—Cont.

Glidden Co., 900 Union Commerce Bldg., Cleveland, Ohio 44115

Guardsman Chemical Coatings, Inc., 1350 Steele, Grand Rapids, Mich. 49502

Hooker Chemical Corp., Durez Plastics Div., North Tonawanda, N.Y. 14120

Interchemical Corp., Finishes Div., 1255-T Broad St., Clifton, N.J. 07015

Kalman Floor Co., Inc., 190 E. Post Road, White Plains, N.Y. 10601

Koppers Co., Inc., Tar & Chemical Div., Koppers Bldg., Pittsburgh, Pa. 15219

Pittsburgh Plate Glass Co., Coatings & Resins Div., One Gateway Center, Pittsburgh, Pa. 15222

Reichhold Chemicals Inc., 525 N. Broadway, White Plains, N.Y. 10603

H. H. Robertson Co., 1107 Two Gateway Center, Pittsburgh, Pa. 15222

Rohm & Haas Co., Independence Mall W., Philadelphia, Pa. 19105

Sherwin-Williams Co., 101 Prospect Ave., N.W., Cleveland, Ohio 44115

Union Carbide Corp., Plastics Div., 270 Park Ave., New York, N.Y. 10017

U.S. Rubber Co., Chemical Div., 152 Elm St., Naugatuck, Conn. 06771

11. Urethane

Allied Chemical Corp., National Aniline Div., 61 Broadway, New York, N.Y. 10016

Archer Daniels Midland Co., 733 Marquette Ave., Minneapolis, Minn. 55440

Carboline Co., 328-R Hanley Industrial Court, St. Louis, Mo. 63144

Ceilcote Co., 140 Sheldon Road, Berea, Ohio 44017

Cook Paint & Varnish Co., 1412 Knox, North Kansas City, Mo. 64111

DeSoto Chemical Coatings, Inc., 1800 S. Mt. Prospect Road, Des Plaines, Ill. 60018

Enterprise Paint Mfg. Co., 2841 S. Ashland Ave., Chicago, Ill. 60608

Essex Chemical Corp., BFC Div., 1401 Broad St., Clinton, N.J. 08809

Gates Engineering Div., Glidden Co., 58 Kern Ave., Wilmington, Del. 19899

B. F. Goodrich Chemical Co., 3135-T Euclid Ave., Cleveland, Ohio 44115

Hughson Chemical Co., W. 12th at Green Garden, Erie, Pa. 16512

Jones-Dabney Co., Resins & Chemicals Div., Louisville, Ky. 40208

Manufacturers of Treatments -Cont.

Pittsburgh Plate Glass Co., Coatings & Resins Div., One Gateway Center, Pittsburgh, Pa. 15222

Plas-Chem Corp., 6177 Maple St., St. Louis, Mo. 63130

Reichhold Chemicals, Inc., 525 N. Broadway, White Plains, N.Y. 10603

Spencer Kellogg, Div. of Textron, Inc., 100 Delaware Ave., Buffalo, N.Y. 14240

12. Epoxy*

Ciba Products Co., Div. of Ciba Corp., 556 Morris Ave., Summit, N.J. 07901

Dow Chemical Co., Plastics Div., Midland, Mich. 48640

General Mills, Inc., Chemical Div., S. Kensington Road, Kankakee, Ill. 60901

Jones-Dabney Co., Div. of Celanese Corp., 8411 Hill Blvd., Louisville, Ky. 40208

Reichhold Chemicals Inc., 525 N. Broadway, White Plains, N.Y. 10603

Shell Chemical Co., Div. of Shell Oil Co., 50 W. 50th St., New York, N.Y. 10020

Union Carbide Corp., Plastics Div., 270 Park Ave., New York, N.Y. 10017

R. T. Vanderbilt Co., Inc., 230 Park Ave., New York, N.Y. 10017

13. Neoprene*

E. I. DuPont de Nemours & Co., Inc., Elastomers Dept., Wilmington, Del. 19801

14. Polysulfide*

Thiokol Chemical Corp., 776 N. Clinton Ave., Trenton, N.J. 08638

15. Coal Tar-Epoxy*

Koppers Co., Inc., Tar & Chemical Div., Koppers Bldg., Pittsburgh, Pa. 15219

U.S.S. Chemicals, Div. of U.S. Steel, Grant Bldg., Pittsburgh, Pa. 15219

*Basic material manufacturers are listed instead of formulators.

Manufacturers of Treatments -Cont.

16. Chemical-Resistant Masonry Units and Mortars

A. Masonry Units

Amercoat Corp., 201 N. Berry St., Brea, Calif. 92621

American Olean Tile Co., 1055 Cannon Ave., Lansdale, Pa. 19446

Atlas Minerals and Chemicals Div., The Electric Storage Battery Co.,
121 Norman St., Mertztown, Pa. 19539

Belden Brick Co., 700 Tuscarawas, W., Canton, Ohio 44701

Ceilcote Co., 140 Sheldon Road, Berea, Ohio 44017

Birmingham Clay Products Co., 2316 Fourth Ave. N., Birmingham, Ala. 35204

Carborundum Co., Refractories and Electronics Div., Box 337, Niagara Falls,
N.Y. 14302

Charlestown Clay Products Co., 6 E. Virginia St., Charlestown, W. Va. 25301

General Refractories Co., 1520 Locust St., Philadelphia, Pa. 19102

Great Lakes Carbon Corp., 18 E. 48th St., New York, N.Y. 10017

A. P. Green Fire Brick Co., 1108 E. Breckenridge St., Mexico, Mo. 65265

Hanley Co., 691 Summerville St., Summerville, Pa. 15864

Harbison-Walker Refractories Co., 2 Gateway Center, Pittsburgh, Pa. 15222

Interpace Corrosion Control Div., Electro-Chemical Engineering and
Manufacturing, 750 Broad St., Emmaus, Pa. 18049

Maurice A. Knight Co., 171 Kelly Ave., Akron, Ohio 44309

KTS Industries, 508 Harrison St., Kalamazoo, Mich. 49006

Milliken Brick Co., 2100 Montier St., Pittsburgh, Pa. 15221

National Carbon Co., Div. of Union Carbide Corp., 270 Park Ave., New York,
N.Y. 10017

Quigley Co., Inc., 415 Madison Ave., New York, N.Y. 10017

Richland Shale Brick Co., P.O. Box 328, Mansfield, Ohio 44901

Rulon Co., Div. of Colonial Industries, Inc., Linwood & Pine Aves.,
Maple Shade, N.J. 08052

Sauereisen Cements Co., RIDC Industrial Park, O'Hara Township, Pittsburgh,
Pa. 15238

Manufacturers of Treatments -Cont.

Stonhard Co., One Park Ave., Maple Shade, N.J. 08052

Summitville Tiles, Inc., Summitville, Ohio 43962

U.S. Stoneware Co., 5300 E. Tallmadge Ave., Akron, Ohio 44309

Watkins Brick Co., P.O. Box B, Birmingham, Ala. 35218

B. Mortars

Amercoat Corp., 201 N. Berry St., Brea, Calif. 92621

Atlas Minerals and Chemicals Div., The Electric Storage Battery Co., 121 Norman St., Mertztown, Pa. 19539

Ceilcote Co., 140 Sheldon Road, Berea, Ohio 44017

Charlotte Chemical Laboratories, Inc., 5046 Old Pineville Road, Charlotte, N.C. 28210

Great Lakes Carbon Corp., 18 E. 48th St., New York, N.Y. 10017

Interpace Corrosion Control Div., Electro-Chemical Engineering and Manufacturing, 750 Broad St., Emmaus, Pa. 18049

Maurice A. Knight Co., 171 Kelly Ave., Akron, Ohio 44309

National Carbon Co., Div. of Union Carbide Corp., 270 Park Ave., New York, N.Y. 10017

Pennsalt Chemicals Corp., Natrona, Pa. 15065

Pittsburgh Plate Glass Co., 223 Belleville Ave., Bloomfield, N.J. 07003

Quigley Co., Inc., 415 Madison Ave., New York, N.Y. 10017

Rulon Co., Div. of Colonial Industries, Inc., Linwood & Pine Aves., Maple Shade, N.J. 08052

Saureisen Cements Co., RIDC Industrial Park, O'Hara Township, Pittsburgh, Pa. 15238

Stebbins Engineering and Mfg. Co., Semco Bldg., Watertown, N.Y.

Sternson, Ltd., Div. of G. F. Sterne & Sons, 126 Bruce St., P.O. Box 130, Brantford, Ont., Can.

Manufacturers of Treatments – Cont.

Stonhard Co., One Park Ave., Maple Shade, N.J. 08052

U.S. Stoneware Co., 5300 E. Tallmadge Ave., Akron, Ohio 44309

17. Sheet Rubber

Amercoat Corp., 201 N. Barry St., Brea, Calif. 92621

Atlas Minerals and Chemicals Div., The Electric Storage Battery Co.,
121 Norman St., Mertztown, Pa. 19539

Boston Woven Hose & Rubber Div., American Biltrite Rubber Co., Inc.
29 Hampshire St., Cambridge, Mass.

Ceilcote Co., 140 Sheldon Road, Berea, Ohio 44017

Enjay Chemical Co., 60 W. 49th St., New York, N.Y. 10020

Gates Engineering Div., Glidden Co., 58 Kern Ave., Wilmington, Del. 19899

Gates Rubber Co., 999 S. Broadway, Denver, Colo. 80217

Goodall Rubber Co., 493 Whitehead Road, Trenton, N.J. 08604

B. F. Goodrich Industrial Products Co., 500 S. Main, Akron, Ohio 44318

Goodyear Tire & Rubber Co., Inc., Industrial Products Div., 1144 E. Market St.,
Akron, Ohio 44316

Heil Process Equipment Corp., 12950 Elmwood Ave., Cleveland, Ohio 44011

Interpace Corrosion Control Div., International Pipe & Ceramics Corp.,
750 Broad St., Emmaus, Pa. 18049

Pennsalt Chemicals Corp., Natrona, Pa. 15065

Rysgaard-Master Co., 1260 W. Connelly, St. Paul, Minn. 51122

U.S. Rubber Co., 1232 Avenue of the Americas, New York, N.Y. 10020

U.S. Stoneware Co., 5300 E. Tallmadge Ave., Akron, Ohio 44309

18. Resin Sheets

Amercoat Corp., 201 N. Berry St., Brea, Calif. 92621

Atlas Minerals and Chemicals Div., The Electric Storage Battery Co.,
121 Norman St., Mertztown, Pa. 19539

Carboline Co. 328-R Hanely Industrial Court, St. Louis, Mo. 63144

Manufacturers of Treatments -Cont.

Ceilcote Co., 140 Sheldon Road, Berea, Ohio 44017

Gates Engineering Div., Glidden Co., 58 Kern Ave., Wilmington, Del. 19899

B. F. Goodrich Industrial Products Co., 500 S. Main, Akron, Ohio 44318

Heil Process Equipment Corp., 12950 Elmwood Ave., Cleveland, Ohio 44011

Interpace Corrosion Control Div., International Pipe & Ceramics Corp.,
750 Broad St., Emmaus, Pa. 18049

Maurice A. Knight Co., 171 Kelly Ave., Akron, Ohio 44309

Rulon Co., Div. of Colonial Industries, Inc., Linwood & Pine Aves.,
Maple Shade, N.J. 08052

U.S. Rubber Co., Royalite Plastic Products, 2634 N. Pulaski Road, Chicago,
Ill. 60639

U.S. Stoneware Co., 5300 E. Tallmadge Ave., Akron, Ohio 44309

19. Lead Sheet

Commercially available locally

20. Glass

Ceramco, Inc. Chemists, 171 Ridge St., Newark, N.J. 07104

Corning Glass Works, Technical Products Div., 80 Houghton Park, Corning,
N.Y. 14830

Owens-Illinois, Inc., Consumer and Technical Products Div., Toledo, Ohio 43601

Pfaudler Co., Div. of Ritter Pfaudler Corp., West Ave. & Clark St., Rochester,
N.Y. 14630

• Pittsburgh Plate Glass Co., 632 Fort Duquesne Blvd., Pittsburgh, Pa. 15222

IX

DESIGN FACTORS

The builder should review his requirements before deciding on a boat design. On-board space, equipment, etc., would vary according to planned use of the boat. The initial cost and maintenance expense of a 40-footer would not be justified for those planning only an occasional sail. Permanent on-board living, or prestige weekend entertaining would require a large size boat. In any event, ponder the needs that are valid and proceed from there.

Most yacht designers and experienced sailors tell us that, normally, two people can handle a sailboat up to 38 feet in length with a reasonable amount of safety. Larger boats will require one or more additional crew members. They also require larger budgets, of course, for initial cost, maintenance and docking.

The boat plans that are offered in this chapter were picked for their ability to satisfy a range of needs, from that of the cruising enthusiast, the weekend sailor, deep-sea fisherman, power cruiser man with a family, on down to the occasional day sailor.

A wooden-boat design for ferro-cement is suggested for one important reason — that of cost. For a great majority, the cost of a yacht designer's plan would not be justified. The average yacht designer will usually charge anywhere from one percent to five percent of the total cost of the boat (usually around $200 to $350 and up), with the stipulation that only one boat may be built from that particular set of plans.

A modest outlay for wooden boat plans provides tried and proven design that will perform safely. Confidence gained by using the boat will help determine future needs. This is the time to consult the professional yacht designer to get the next boat tailored to exact needs and desires. At that time his fee will be money well spent. Several yacht designers and builders are listed later in this chapter for those persons desiring to have someone else design or build their ferro-cement boat.

Hull Thickness

When comparing the weight of a ferro-cement hull with that of a similar wooden hull, remember both will be the same weight at around the 30-foot length. If one progresses beyond the 30-foot length, then the ferro-cement hull becomes some five percent lighter than a similar wooden one. Going the other way, the ferro-cement rapidly gets heavier than wood, unless one uses less hull thickness. The average hull thickness for this discussion will be about one inch, though on hulls smaller than 30 feet one can certainly go to a thinner hull.

Ferro-cement hulls larger than 30 feet in workboats, power cruisers, or sailboats are most economical to build when compared to wood, steel, aluminum or fiberglas. Ferro-cement gives an increase of interior space when compared to wood construction, something on the order of 12 percent. This is due, of course, to the elimination of thick beams and frames, and to greater planking thickness, especially in larger hull sizes.

Hull thickness can be varied for hulls that are under 30 feet. This is done because of the weight factor. Example:

A 16-foot boat with approximately 150 square feet of hull surface area. The steel and concrete weight for one-square foot of hull area is 12 pounds, for a hull thickness of one inch. Total square footage times weight per square foot equals total hull weight (150 square feet x 12 pounds per square feet = 1,800 pounds).

Suppose a hull thickness of 5/8 inch is desired, how much weight should be eliminated?

Divide the one-inch-thick, square foot of hull area by eight to determine just what a 1/8-inch-thick, one-square-foot section would weigh (12 pounds ÷ 8 = 1.5 pounds per square foot). So if a 5/8-inch thickness is desired, multiply 1.5 pounds by 5 and have 7.5 pounds for a 5/8-inch-thick square foot of hull.

Then multiply 150 square feet by 7.5 pounds and get a total weight of 1,125 pounds. Subtracting 1,125 pounds from 1,800 pounds gives us a 675 pounds saving in weight. Such a hull would have a superior strength factor over a wooden or fiberglas hull. A 5/8-inch-thick hull would be constructed by eliminating the 1/4-inch spacing rods and using the maximum layers of 18-gauge, one-inch diamond-shaped chicken wire, as called for in Fig. 2-7.

Floating docks call for the conventional one-inch-thick hulls to help absorb high-impact loads from docking boats. Both vertical and horizontal spacing rods should be used, along with the necessary layers of mesh.

The hull thickness on the *Marco Polo*, described in Chapter VI, is just over one inch. Some interesting facts come to light when the weight of the steel content in the *Marco Polo* is reviewed. The steel rods placed vertically and horizontally on three-inch centers required eight feet of rods per square foot. The steel rod weighed 0.167 pounds per foot; this gave a weight of 1.336 pounds of rod per square foot. The plasterer's lath weighed about 0.264 pounds per square foot; and three layers were used for a total mesh weight of 0.792 pounds per sqaure foot. The total of the two is 2.128 pounds per square foot, which falls within the desired steel content range of two-to-three pounds of steel per square foot of hull area.

Naval Architects — Ferro-Cement

L. Hedges
60 Caringbah Road
Caringbah, N.S.W.-2229, Australia

Marine Design Enterprises
414 Blundell Road
Richmond, B.C., Canada

James C. Catalano
26 Lorelei Lane
Menlo Park, Calif. 94025, USA

Holland Marine Design
2555 Park Blvd.
Palo Alto, Calif. 94306, USA

L. Francis Herreshoff
The Castle
Marblehead, Mass., USA

G. L. Watson and Co.
9 North Drive
Glasgow C 1, Scotland

Boatbuilders—Ferro-Cement

Crowley's Boatshed
57 McConnel Street
Bulimba, Qld. 4171, Australia

Redwood Ferro-Crete
1552 Maple Street
Redwood City, Calif. 94063, USA

Fiber Steel Corp.
P.O. Box 661
W. Sacramento, Calif., 95691, USA

Windboats, Ltd.
Wroxham, Norwich
Norfolk, England

Ferro-Cement Marine Services
7 Ship Road
Burnham on Crouch
Essex, England

BOAT PLANS

The designs on pages 102, and 106—108 are examples of hulls designed originally for wood and are readily adaptable to ferro-cement construction. Those on pages 103—105 are hulls designed for ferro-cement construction. Full-scale plans for PELICAN, KITTIWAKE and PICAROON are available through any book dealer or Cornell Maritime Press, Inc., Box 109, Cambridge, Maryland 21613.

PELICAN: Auxiliary Cruiser 24' Long; 9'0" Beam; 3'6" Draft; Sail Area 260 Sq. Ft. (Scale: 1" = 1') (7 Sheets).
$14.00

PELICAN
24 FT AUXILIARY CRUISER
SAIL PLAN & PROFILE

16'-0"

50 SQ.FT.

6'-6"

14'-0"

14'-6"

9'-6"

155 SQ.FT.

265 SQ.FT.

110 SQ.FT.

1'-0"

11'-6"

23'-0"

14'-0"

60.SQ.FT.

7'-3"

17'-0"

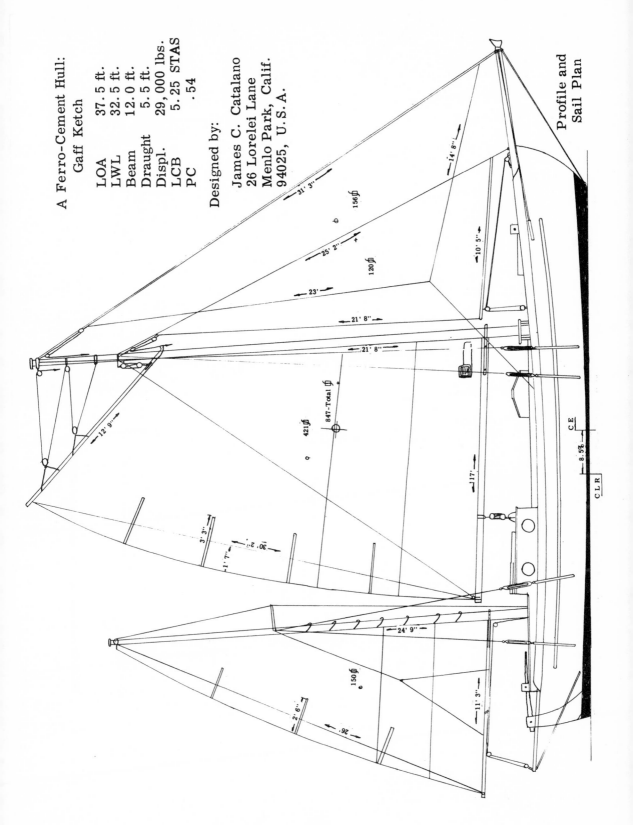

A Ferro-Cement Hull:
Gaff Ketch

LOA   37.5 ft.
LWL   32.5 ft.
Beam   12.0 ft.
Draught 5.5 ft.
Displ.   29,000 lbs.
LCB   5.25 STAS
PC   .54

Designed by:

James C. Catalano
26 Lorelei Lane
Menlo Park, Calif.
94025, U.S.A.

Profile and
Sail Plan

31' 3"

14' 8"

25' 2"

156 ☐

120 ☐

10' 5"

23'

21' 8"

21' 8"

847-Total ☐

421 ☐

12' 9"

CE

8.5%

C L R

117'

3' 3"

30' 2"

1' 7"

24' 9"

150 ☐

11' 3"

2' 6"

26'

103

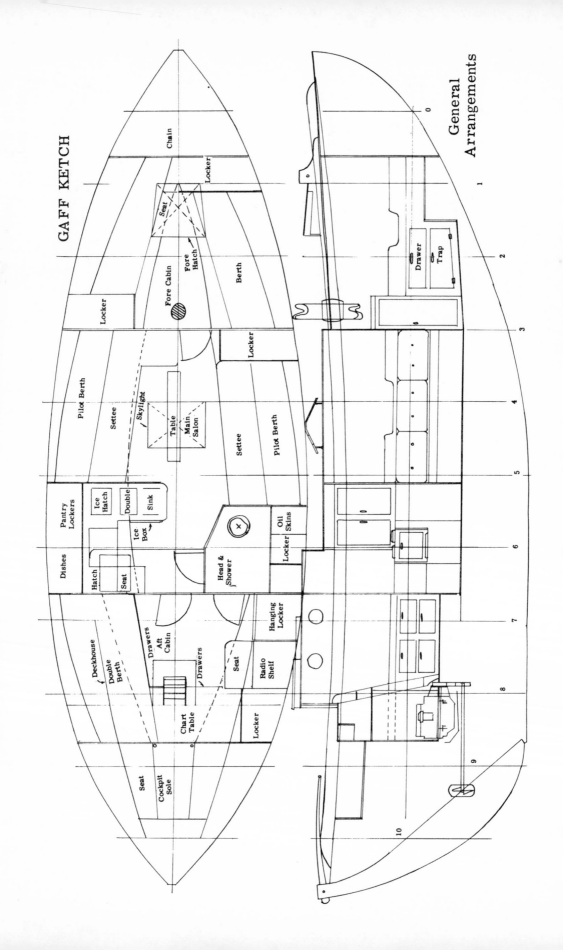

GAFF KETCH

General Arrangements

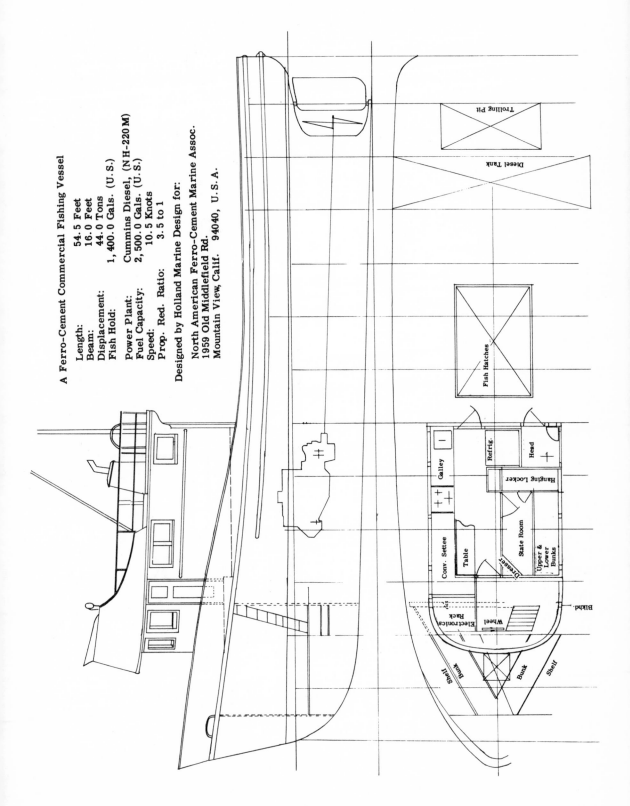

A Ferro-Cement Commercial Fishing Vessel

Length:	54.5 Feet
Beam:	16.0 Feet
Displacement:	44.0 Tons
Fish Hold:	1,400.0 Gals. (U.S.)
Power Plant:	Cummins Diesel, (NH-220 M)
Fuel Capacity:	2,500.0 Gals. (U.S.)
Speed:	10.5 Knots
Prop. Red. Ratio:	3.5 to 1

Designed by Holland Marine Design for:

North American Ferro-Cement Marine Assoc.
1959 Old Middlefield Rd.
Mountain View, Calif. 94040, U.S.A.

Trolling Pit

Diesel Tank

Fish Hatches

Refrig.

Head

Galley

Hanging Locker

Conv. Settee

State Room

Table

Dresser

Upper & Lower Bunks

Wheel

Electronics Rack

Blkhd.

Shelf

Bunk

Bunk

Shelf

105

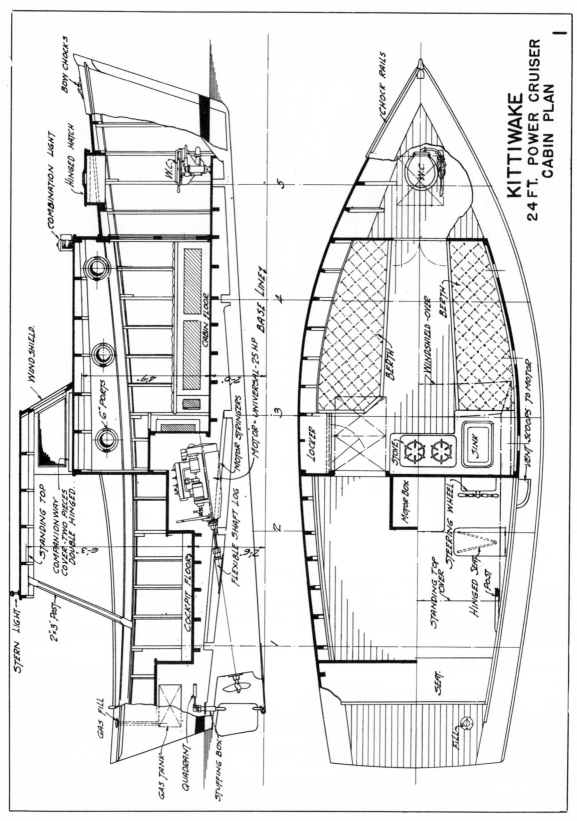

KITTIWAKE
24 FT. POWER CRUISER
CABIN PLAN

106

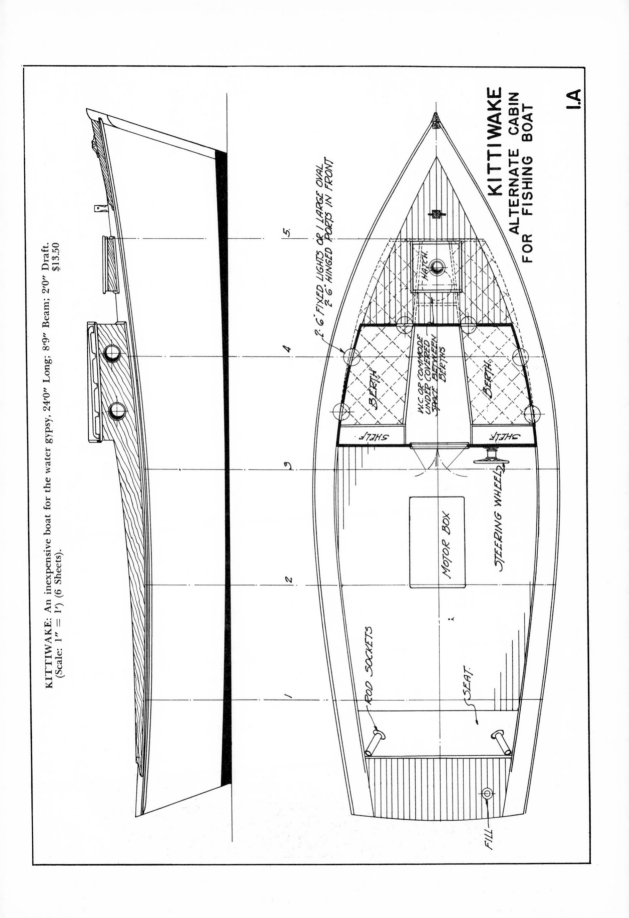

KITTIWAKE: An inexpensive boat for the water gypsy, 24'0" Long; 8'9" Beam; 2'0" Draft.
(Scale: 1" = 1') (6 Sheets). $13.50

KITTIWAKE
ALTERNATE CABIN
FOR FISHING BOAT

I.A

2' 6' FIXED LIGHTS OR 1 LARGE OVAL
2' 6' HINGED PORTS IN FRONT

HATCH.

W.C. OR COMMODE
UNDER COVERED
SPACE BETWEEN
BERTHS

BERTH

BERTH

SHELF

SHELF

STEERING WHEEL

MOTOR BOX

ROD SOCKETS

SEAT.

FILL

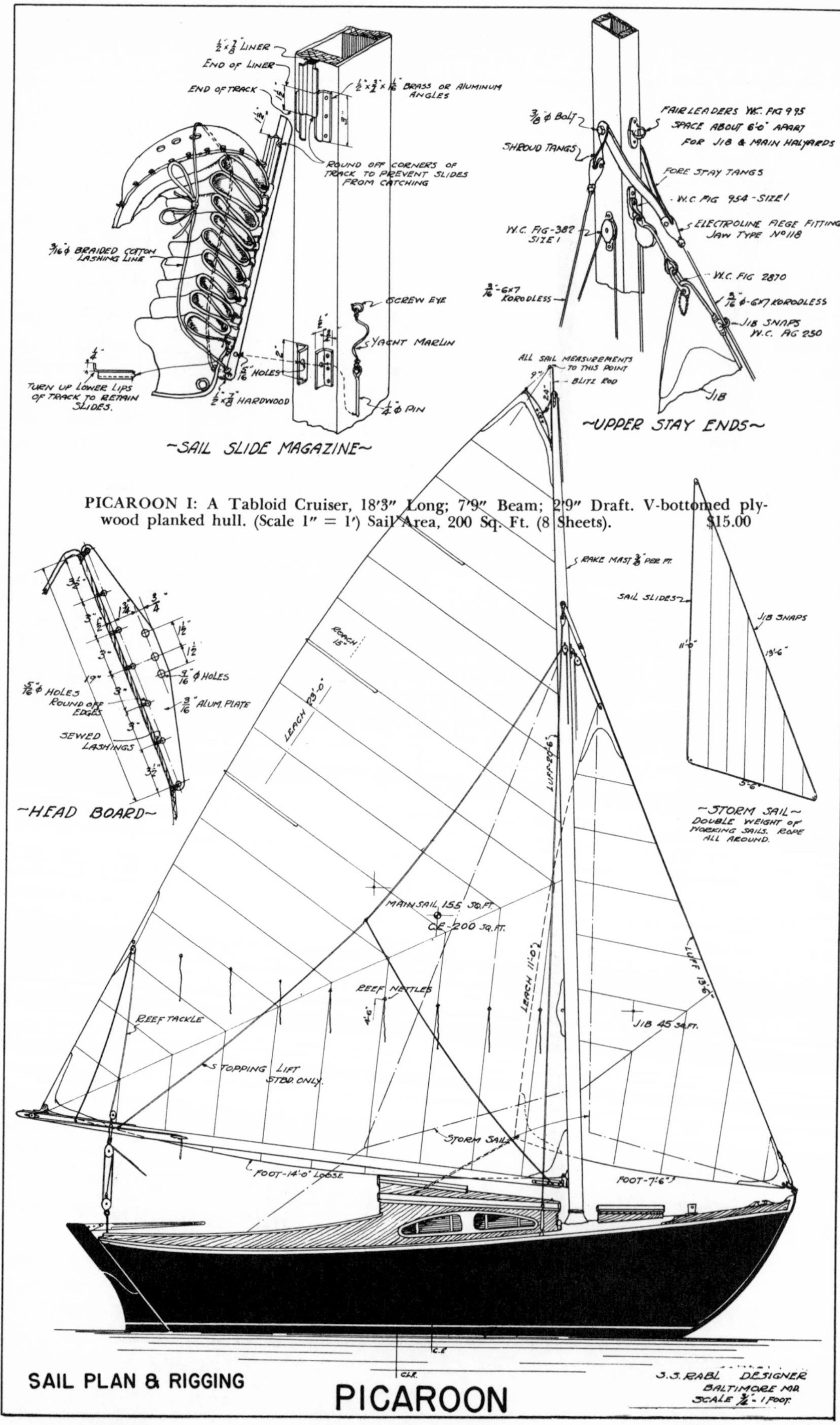

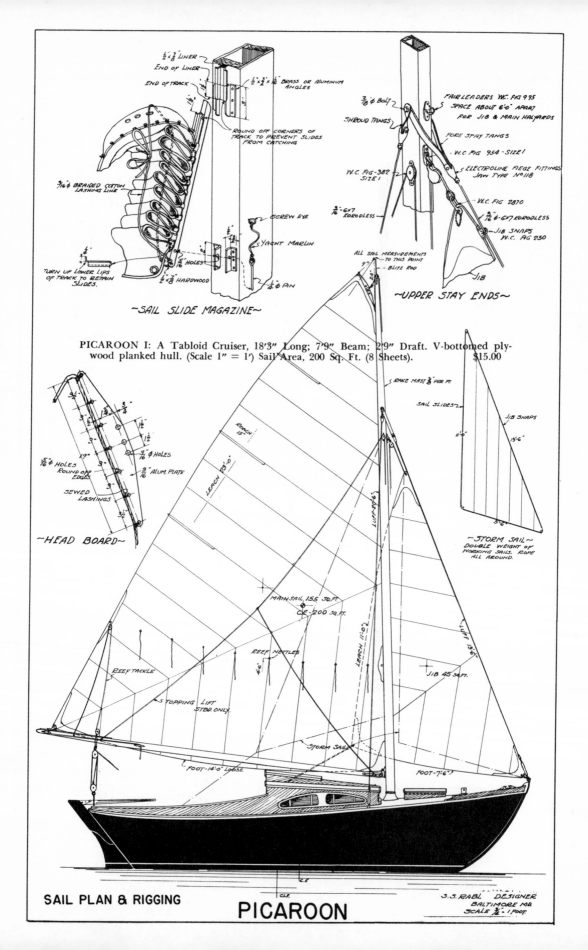

½ x ⅞ LINER
END OF LINER
END OF TRACK
½ x ½ x 1/16 BRASS OR ALUMINUM ANGLES
ROUND OFF CORNERS OF TRACK TO PREVENT SLIDES FROM CATCHING
3/16 ϕ BRAIDED COTTON LASHING LINE
SCREW EYE
YACHT MARLIN
5/16" HOLES
TURN UP LOWER LIPS OF TRACK TO RETAIN SLIDES.
½ x ⅞ HARDWOOD
¼ ϕ PIN
~SAIL SLIDE MAGAZINE~
⅜ ϕ BOLT
SHROUD TANGS
FAIR LEADERS W.C. FIG 995 SPACE ABOUT 6'0" APART FOR JIB & MAIN HALYARDS
FORE STAY TANGS
W.C. FIG 954 - SIZE 1
ELECTROLINE FIEGE FITTINGS JAW TYPE No 118
W.C. FIG-382 SIZE 1
W.C. FIG 2870
3/16 - 6x7 KORODLESS
3/16 ϕ - 6x7 KORODLESS
JIB SNAPS W.C. FIG 250
JIB
~UPPER STAY ENDS~
ALL SAIL MEASUREMENTS TO THIS POINT
BLITZ ROD
RAKE MAST ⅜ PER FT.
SAIL SLIDES
JIB SNAPS
~STORM SAIL~
DOUBLE WEIGHT OF WORKING SAILS. ROPE ALL AROUND.
9/16 ϕ HOLES
5/16 ϕ HOLES ROUND OFF EDGES
3/16 ALUM. PLATE
SEWED LASHINGS
~HEAD BOARD~
ROACH 15"
LEACH 23'-0"
LUFF 20'-6"
MAINSAIL 155 SQ.FT.
C.E. 200 SQ.FT.
REEF NETTLES
REEF TACKLE
STOPPING LIFT STBD. ONLY.
LEACH 11'-0"
LUFF 15'-6"
JIB 45 SQ.FT.
STORM SAIL
FOOT-14'-0" LOOSE
FOOT-7'-6"
C.L.R.
SAIL PLAN & RIGGING
PICAROON
S.S. RABL DESIGNER BALTIMORE MD.
SCALE ¾" - 1 FOOT.

PICAROON I: A Tabloid Cruiser, 18′3″ Long; 7′9″ Beam; 2′9″ Draft. V-bottomed plywood planked hull. (Scale 1″ = 1′) Sail Area, 200 Sq. Ft. (8 Sheets). $15.00

X

TESTING AND INSPECTION

For those builders wishing to have their boats classified in any of the various shipping registers, a positive testing and inspection program must be followed during construction. The program's documentation should be submitted to the local surveyor as specified by his register's rules and regulations.

Before any work commences on the hull, complete plans, materials list, and specifications must be submitted to the register for approval by its staff of marine engineers. As in the case of *Lloyd's Register of Shipping*, each particular set of plans and specifications will be approved on an individual basis.

In planning an adequate inspection system, one must have an initial conference with the register's local surveyor. This enables the builder and the surveyor to agree upon the proposed inspection system and to approve the choice of a reputable testing laboratory.

One engineer, A. L. Edge, Technical Department, Cement Marketing Co. Ltd., London, commented to me that, "It's almost impossible to distinguish between a good or poor quality ferro-cement hull after it has been finished."

Hence the need for the builder to insure that he has made all the necessary representative test panels, and collected sufficient numbered mortar test cylinders so that certified tests can be made. Then, if the question ever arises, the quality of the hull is known. This is particularly necessary when contemplating selling the craft through a reputable yacht broker.

Inspections should be conducted at these intervals:

1. When the steel reinforcement (mesh and rods) is half completed.

2. When the final layers of mesh reinforcement are completed and the hull securely wired.

3. During the application of mortar.

4. At the stripping of form work (if any).

5. At the end of the curing period.

Black-and-white or color photographs are highly recommended and should be taken with a Polaroid camera, and immediately certified, with the following information noted on the back: hull number, design series name, date, time and phase of construction, with the builder's signature. These photos, along with representative test panels, mortar test cylinders, and results of slump tests, form a permanent part of the boat's documents.

Test results that must be certified by a reputable testing laboratory cover the following items:

1. Sample representative panels, laid up from the same materials and mix, and reinforced with the same kind and number of rods and layers of wire mesh as used on the hull, are to be prepared and tested to determine the typical mechanical properties of the ferro-cement. Flexural and impact strengths must be made on reinforced panels, but tensile and compressive strengths may be obtained from un-reinforced materials.

109

2. Compression tests of a suitable number of test cubes or cylinders are to be taken and numbered (the lowest number denoting the start of the plastering operation, the highest the end) during the course of application of the mortar. These tests will be considered as being representative of the material being used in construction of the hull. Note: These samples must either be filled in the presence of the surveyor or by an employee or official of the testing laboratory that has been retained to test the panels and test cylinders. Samples are to be cured and tested at the 7th and 28th day cure points.

3. Slump testing of various mortar mixes is to be conducted prior to mixing and application of mortar. This is done to find out which mix will have good workability with the least amount of water content. Slump testing is accomplished by placing the trial batch in a standard slump cone (as provided by the testing laboratory). Compact or rod the mix for a specified amount of time, then remove the cone quickly and measure the amount of "slump" that has occurred at the very top of the mix, as opposed to the known height of the slump cone. The more the slump, the more the water content. Thus it is possible to compare mixes against each other by varying the water content of otherwise similar mixes. This method is used widely in the building industry as a check to verify that a batch of mortar does not have an excessive amount of water content. This test complements the careful measuring and mixing procedures discussed in Chapter V.

4. Watertightness of the hull must be checked, either by actual floating or filling. A sound, smooth surface will be assumed to be watertight until actually tested.

The above items are intended to be a general guide to the builder, so that the primary information will be documented before, during and after hull construction. The surveyor will have more items that must be considered, such as installation of decks, bulkheads, machinery, etc. that are not of ferro-cement. These items must be in accordance with current rules applicable to the particular item or material used.

Lloyd's Register of Shipping has established tentative requirements for ferro-cement hulls and issued these under Technical Note FC/REQ/1, dated 2nd January, 1967, entitled: "Tentative Requirements for the Construction of Yachts and Small Craft in Ferro-Cement." This can be obtained by writing to *Lloyd's Register of Shipping*, London, E.C. 3, England.

Generally speaking, once a boat has been certified for inclusion into the register, it will have a special mark preceding its name, to denote that it is constructed of ferro-cement. An annual survey must then be carried out by a surveyor who is certified to survey ferro-cement hulls.

For builders residing in the Commonwealth, the following list of British Standards Institute publications are referred to in *Lloyd's "Tentative Requirements for the Construction of Yachts and Small Craft in Ferro-Cement."*

B.S. 18, *Tensile Testing of Materials*

B.S. 735, Part 1 and Part 2, dated 1964, *Specifications for Hot Rolled Bars and Hard Drawn Wire*

B.S. 1881, *Curing of Concrete Samples for Compressive Testing*

C.P. 114, dated 1957, paragraphs 306–308, "Practices for Mixing, Handling, Compaction and Curing of Concrete"

P.D. 6031, dated December, 1968, 2nd edition, "The Use of the Metric System in the Construction Industry"

These booklets can be obtained at a reasonable price by writing to the British Standards Institution, British Standards House, 2, Park Street, London W 1, England (telegrams: Standards London W 1; telephone: 01-629-9000).

American and Canadian builders can reference the A.S.T.M. codes, and by writing to either the American Concrete Institute, Detroit, Michigan, or to the Portland Cement Association, Skokie, Illinois, for more specific standards. Another agency to write to is the U.S. Coast Guard, Washington, D.C., for possible tentative standards. As of 1970, I do not know of any standards for ferro-cement that have been established, except for those of *Lloyd's Register of Shipping*.

Following sound practices and testing procedures assures the builder of having a high-quality ferro-cement hull.

XI

ENGINEERING REPORTS

"An Investigation of 'Ferro-Cement' Using Expanded Metal"

By J. G. Byrne and W. Wright*

One of the main reasons why ferro-cement has not hitherto been used much outside Italy is undoubtedly the high cost of the woven steel mesh used by Prof. Nervi. To overcome this objection the authors have investigated, at the Engineering School of Trinity College, Dublin, similar material using expanded metal in place of woven steel mesh, because expanded metal is less expensive. Initially, the investigation was undertaken to verify that the material would be suitable for a roof canopy which has since been published elsewhere, as also has a description of the canopy. The result of further research work is reported in the following.

The Mortar

In the investigation, a mortar similar to that used by Prof. Nervi was used, except in the case of some shrinkage tests. The cement-sand ratio was 0.7 and the water-cement ratio was 0.4. The cement was rapid-hardening portland cement of Irish manufacture. An apparently workable mortar was provided, in that it did not contain too much sand for passing a No. 100 B.S. sieve. This mixture is very rich since it contains about 1250-lbs. of cement per cubic yard. Consequently, the set mortar has high tensile and compressive strengths, the former being about 500 to 600-lbs. per square inch and the latter about 6,000 to 7,000-lbs. per square inch as measured on 4-in. cubes at seven days. Thus it has the desirable property that accompanies high strength, that is, exceptionally high resistance to cracking, but it has a low density of about 133-lbs. per cubic foot.

Another advantage of a rich mixture is the high quality of the finished surface. It is difficult to expel all the air from such a mixture by vibration or other means, but tests showed that satisfactory results could be obtained merely by placing the mortar in a mold and that nothing was gained by attempting to compact it further. The mortar was virtually impermeable, as would be expected from the results obtained by Lecznar and Oskroba, who have shown that this is the case if the surface area of the aggregate, as is so with ferro-cement mortars. Because of this, ferro-cement roofing units are used in Italy without asphalt or other protection, but in the climate prevailing in the British Isles this is not practicable since the durability of the mortar against attrition due to rain and abrasion is not high.

In addition to poor durability, the main disadvantages of the mortar appear to be high shrinkage and creep. Comparative shrinkage tests of 6-inch by 12-inch cylinders were carried out on materials ranging from neat cement to 3:1 sand-cement mortars with a water-cement ratio of 0.35. The shrinkage, which was measured on an 8-inch

*Reprinted with permission of Concrete Publication, Ltd., *Concrete and Constructional Engineering*, Vol. LVI, No. 12 (December, 1961).

Demac strain gauge, is given in Fig. 11-1. This clearly shows that the cement-sand ratio has a predominating effect and the water-cement ratio very little effect. For a low water-cement ratio of 0.35 the shrinkage appears to be low despite the high cement content. (The mixture used by Prof. Nervi has a water-cement ratio of 0.35 and is quite workable and plastic if the sand is not too fine.) The sand was very fine and a water-cement ratio of 0.4 gave improved workability and much more shrinkage. No creep tests were carried out but it generally follows that the same factors affect shrinkage and creep alike. From the point of view of shrinkage and creep only, the best

Water-cement ratio	0.35	0.40	0.40	0.40	0.45	0.50	0.55	0.50	0.55
Cement-sand ratio	Neat	0.70	0.60	0.50	0.40	0.40	0.40	0.33	0.33
Shrinkage	84	71	63	44	57	57	53	47	45

Fig. 11-1. Shrinkage of ferro-cement.

mortar has a water-cement ratio of 0.55 and a cement-sand ratio of 0.33, but these are not necessarily the best ratios from other points of view. The resistance of this mortar to cracking due to shrinkage is about the same as the resistance to cracking of the mortar used in this investigation because of its greater tensile strength. Thus, the only undesirable consequences of using a rich mortar are the increased deflections due to shrinkage and creep.

The Steel Mesh

Prof. Nervi uses a light-gauge square wire-mesh which costs about 2s, 4d. per lb. in Ireland; expanded metal is about half the price. There are no disadvantages in the use of expanded metal, and there are some advantages such as good mechanical bond, ease of placing and few layers are needed whatever the amount required. It should, however, be noted that during a tensile test with 1/2-in. expanded metal mesh weighing 4.77 lbs. per square yard, the mortar split badly due to a scissors action of the diamond mesh, thus indicating that there is a limit to the size and weight of the mesh. A 3/4-in. mesh weighing 1.67-lbs. per square yard and a 1-in. mesh up to 2.5-lbs. per square yard proved satisfactory. It is difficult to measure the tensile strength of expanded metal in the condition as delivered, but an apparatus which was devised to measure the tensile strength of ferro-cement and which has been described elsewhere proved suitable for measuring the strength of the mesh. The expanded metal is embedded in mortar and a thin piece of cardboard is inserted in the middle; this is easily picked out after the mortar has been cured in water for seven days. The mean tensile strength was found to be 24.6 tons per square inch for clean mesh and 22.4 tons per square inch for steel slightly rusty.

The Behaviour of the Ferro-Cement

Ferro-cement behaves in a similar manner to reinforced concrete and the strength of members is calculated in the same way. The fact that a light, well distributed mesh is used gives some advantages over ordinary reinforced concrete in that the widths of the cracks are much less and the distribution of the cracks more favorable. This helps to counteract the adverse effect the small cover of mortar might have on the corrosion of the steel, which is generally thought to be the main disadvantage of ferro-cement. Tests carried out by Miss R. Friedland show that the most important factor in the protection of the steel is a dense plastic cement paste of good quality. The cover has an effect only when the quality of the cement paste is not good, that is, when there is too little cement, too much water and insufficient compaction. This is therefore a good reason for using a rich mortar such as used by Prof. Nervi.

The main criterion in the design of structures containing light thin elements is the limitation of deflection due to shrinkage and creep. An advantage of the mesh is that deflections due to shrinkage are reduced, since the mesh is distributed in a reasonably uniform manner. Two specimens, each 2-in. by 4-in. by 3/4-in., were tested under half the cracking load; one had two layers of mesh and the other had none. The latter specimen deflected 0.023 initially and after two months the deflection was 0.070. The specimen with mesh had a similar initial deflection, but the deflection after two months was 0.095. This larger increase in the reinforced specimen is due to the fact that the steel mesh was placed unsymmetrically, but it is much less than the increase that would be obtained if the reinforcement consisted of a few bars. An unloaded specimen with mesh deflected 0.023. It might be possible to place the mesh in such a way say, by casting the specimens with the tension side uppermost and ensuring that the centre of gravity of the steel is nearer the compression (face) than the deflections due to shrinkage could be reduced considerably. This, in the opinion of the authors, is one of the two main functions of the steel in ferro-cement units.

Ferro-cement seems to be suitable mainly for small mass-produced precast units which are loaded in compression, and the method of construction used by Prof. Nervi is such that the maximum stresses are not great. It seems to the authors that one way to regard the steel is as providing protection against complete collapse if cracks occur. The ultimate resistance should be regarded as the tensile strength of the mortar for members subject to tension. Steel equivalent to the cracking load should be provided and, for design purposes, the working load should be taken as equal to half the cracking load. This definition of working stress should ensure that there is no corrosion in favorable atmospheres, and deflection should not be excessive. The most economical method of design might be to consider the working load as equal to the cracking load, thereby making sure that steel is capable of providing adequate ultimate resistance. The latter method has been employed by the Irish Electricity Supply Board, who have used thin ferro-cement slabs in place of steel cover plates on ducts. The slabs are about 33-in. square and 1-in. thick and have three layers of expanded metal. Four of these slabs were tested and the results were satisfactory; the equivalent uniformly-distributed load at failure over a 29-in. span was 1,000-lbs. per square foot, which is greater than specified. The deflection at failure was large, being about 1-1/2-inches, but this is an advantage since there would be ample visual warning of failure. The working load specified was 150-lbs. per square foot, and the initial deflection at this load was about 1/450 of the span. By placing one layer of steel near the bottom and two near the compression zone, adequate ultimate resistance and considerable reduction of deflection due to shrinkage is ensured.

Apart from doubts about durability, the main objection to ferro-cement is probably the cost. The first cost of the material is certainly high, but if an efficient method of construction is used, this can largely be overcome. Ferro-cement is generally used for small identical units so that only a few accurate molds would have to be made. Skilled craftsmen are required to make the molds and also to finish the actual products.

The authors wish to thank Mr. L.D.G. Collen, who initiated the investigation described, and Mr. E. J. Flight, Technical Director of the Expanded Metal Co., for his advice and support.

"Some Notes on the Characteristics of Ferro-Cement"

By Lyal D. G. Collen, M.A.I., M.I.C.E.I. and R. W. Kirwan, M.A.I., A.M.I.C.E.*

The work of the Italian structural engineer Pier L. Nervi has attracted a great deal of attention and admiration in recent years. Whilst much has been published about his work in broad outline, and the general engineering principles involved in his structures are well illustrated and described, little has been written in detail in English about the mechanical properties of his material, ferro-cement.

Nervi developed ferro-cement in 1943 and used it firstly as a material in naval architecture, then in 1948 he used it in civil engineering and building. In the Cement and Concrete Association translation No. 60, dtd. July 1956, "Ferro-Cement, its characteristics and potentialities," Nervi gives some details of the properties of ferro-cement. He defines ferro-cement as being "thin slabs of mortar reinforced with superimposed layers of wire mesh and small diameter bars giving a product with a high degree of elasticity and resistance to cracking and requiring a minimum of formwork." Nervi continues to describe in detail the proportions of steel, sand and cement which would give optimum results, viz., five quintals of steel and eight to ten quintals of cement per cubic metre (840 lbs. of steel and 1,340 to 1,680 lbs. of cement per cubic yard). These proportions are what Nervi described as the "natural proportions."

The authors, thinking that conditions in the building and civil engineering industries of Italy and Ireland were not dissimilar, each country having a shortage of steel and a surplus of skilled craftsmen, felt that the material has possibilities in the Irish economy. They therefore decided to conduct a series of tests designed to confirm and amplify the information at present available in technical literature in English. The preliminary tests described below were intended as an introduction to the material. More detailed investigation of many aspects is required and it is hoped that this article will encourage further research.

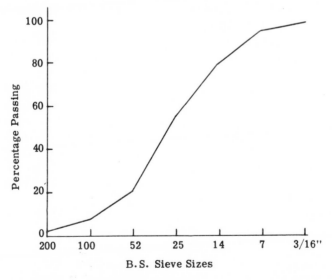

Fig. 11-2. Sand grading curve.

The size of beam chosen was 3-ft. 0-in. long and 5-1/2-in. wide by 1/8-in. deep. This was suited to the 10-ton testing machine available and also bore a fairly close

*Reprinted with permission from *Civil Engineering and Public Works Review* (London: February, 1959).

relationship to the actual thickness of ferro-cement as used in practice. The beams were cast on their flat surfaces in shallow timber moulds. The mortar mix used in the normal tests consisted of 50-lbs. of sand and 28-lbs. of rapid hardening Irish portland cement I.S.S. No. 1 and had a water cement ratio of 0.35. The sand was a sharp washed material from a pit in a terminal moraine in County Kildare, and its grading is shown on the curve in Fig. 11-2.

The test beams were cast by first placing a thin layer of mortar 3/8-in. thick in the mould and then pressing two or three layers of mesh into the mortar, then a second layer of mortar was laid together with the centre 1/4-in. diameter mild steel rods,

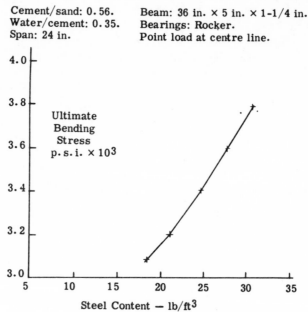

Cement/sand: 0.56. Beam: 36 in. × 5 in. × 1-1/4 in.
Water/cement: 0.35. Bearings: Rocker.
Span: 24 in. Point load at centre line.

Fig. 11-3. Ultimate bending stress against steel content.

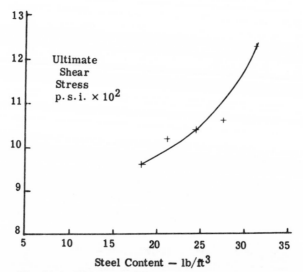

Cement/sand: 0.56. Beam: 5 in. × 1-1/4 in.
Water/cement: 0.35. Bearings: Solid.
Span: 5-3/4 in. U.D.L.: 4-1/2 in. × 4-1/2 in.

Fig. 11-4. Ultimate shear stress against steel content.

followed by the remaining layers of mesh and the last layer of mortar. The mortar was hand mixed and placed with a trowel. Vibration was not used. The beams were covered with damp sacking and were stripped 24 hours later and cured in a tank of water at 51-degrees F. six days before testing.

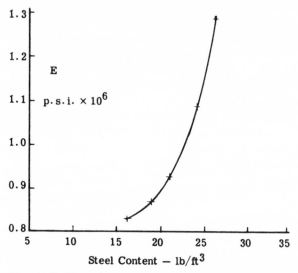

Cement/sand: 0.56.   Beam: 36 in. × 5 in. × 1-1/4 in.
Water/cement: 0.35   Bearings: Rocker.
Span: 24 in.   Point load at centre line.
E calculated from deflections.

Fig. 11-5. Young's modulus (E) against steel content.

Ultimate bending stress against:
(i) variation of cement/sand ratio.
(ii) variation of water/cement ratio.

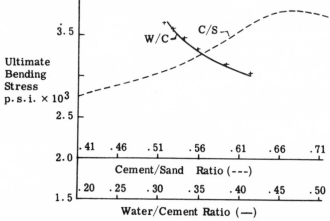

Span: 24 in.   Water/cement ratio in
Beam: 36 in. × 5 in. × 1-1/4 in.   cement/sand tests: 0.35.
Bearings: Rocker.   Cement/sand ratio in water/
Point load at centre line.   cement tests: 9.56.
Steel content constant at 16.1 lb/ft^3.

Fig. 11-6. Ultimate bending stress against variation of cement/sand ratio and variation of water/cement ratio.

The 1-7/8-in. by 1-inch mesh was specially woven in ungalvanized 18 gauge mild steel wire, there being twin wires in the warp and single in the weft. The mesh weighed 1.4-lbs. per square yard (lb./yd.^{2}) and was machine woven. The unusual form with twin wires in the warp was necessary to make the fabric strong enough to withstand handling without resorting to welding or tying.

In Figs. 11-3 and 11-4 are illustrated the results obtained for bending and shear stress when the steel content is varied, the water-cement and cement-sand ratios being kept constant. As one would expect the values increase as the steel content rises. In the case of the bending stress the strength is almost in direct proportion to the quantity of steel. The maximum bending stress of 3,800-lbs per cubic foot. This steel content represents 12 layers of mesh and one row of 1/4-in. diameter bars, in a total depth of 1-1/4-in. This will doubtless be recognized as being close to the maximum practical steel content and therefore the maximum strength with the given cement and water contents. The values for Young's Modulus which were obtained from the measurement of the deflections are shown in Fig. 11-5.

It is interesting to compare the value shown in Figs. 3, 4, and 5 with the basic working stresses for Canadian spruce as published by the Timber Development Association in their booklet "Structural Grading of Timber," bearing in mind that the ferro-cement stresses are ultimate values:

Canadian Spruce Basic Stresses

Bending, 800-lbs. per square inch.
Shear parallel to the grain, 100-lbs. per square inch.
Young's Modulus, 750,000 to 1,200,000-lbs. per square inch.

The effects of variations in the cement/sand and water/cement ratios on the ultimate bending stress are demonstrated in Fig. 11-6. A maximum stress is reached with the cement/sand ratio of 0.66, thereafter the strength falls off. The water/cement ratio is possibly more interesting as it is more critical — quite an appreciable drop in strength as the water content increases. The value of 0.35 which was used in many of the tests provided a workable mix and one which could be readily used under site conditions.

The authors would point out that these tests were exploratory, but they feel that they do demonstrate the possibilities of ferro-cement as a material capable of flexible architectural treatment. There is of course a very wide field for research particularly in the more effective use of the steel, possible in some other form of mesh or even in using a steel of higher tensile strength.

XII

EARLY CONCRETE SHIPS

During World War I an acute shortage of steel existed, and it was suggested that one could build ships and barges using concrete. The Emergency Fleet Building Corporation had been formed by the federal government in an effort to build more ships and barges for the war effort. This corporation proposed building a 7,500-ton concrete ship, which was certainly the biggest concrete vessel proposed up to that time.

The feasibility study was given to a marine engineer, R. J. Wig. He determined that it would not be economically feasible unless one could produce and use concrete having a compressive strength of 5,000 pounds per square inch and a weight per cubic foot of not more than 110 pounds. Thus the search for a lightweight aggregate was undertaken. During this feasibility study Mr. Wig became acquainted with studies being made by H. J. Hayde of Kansas City, Missouri, who was successful in expanding clay and shale into strong, vesicular, lightweight aggregates. The quantities produced were only on a small scale, but Mr. Wig obtained the service of the National Bureau of Standards to determine ways to produce lightweight aggregates in quantity. This program succeeded due to the first lightweight aggregates being produced commercially at Birmingham, Alabama. The Emergency Fleet Building Corporation then contracted with the Atlas Portland Cement Company for the quantity production of expanded shale aggregates.

AVERAGE GRADATION – % Passing		
Sieve	Coarse	Fine
5/8	100.0	
1/2	78.0	
3/16	5.2	99.5
10	0	90.0
20		70.0
40		44.3
60		29.0
80		18.1
100		12.1
AVERAGE UNIT WEIGHT – lb./cu. ft.		
	43.8	69.4

Fig. 12-1. Average unit weights and average gradations of lightweight aggregates.

119

TEST	NO. OF SPECIMENS	MIX PROPORTIONS BY VOL.	MIXING WATER Percentage by Weight	MIXING WATER Gal./Bag	CEMENT Bag/Cu. Yd.	WEIGHT (pcf.) Wet	WEIGHT (pcf.) Sat.	WEIGHT (pcf.) Oven Dry	ABSORPTION %	CONSISTENCY DROP OR SLUMP (in.)	COMPRESSIVE STRENGTH (psi) 7 day	COMPRESSIVE STRENGTH (psi) 28 day	COMPRESSIVE STRENGTH (psi) 34 year	E-VALUE x 10⁻³ (psi)	BOND (psi)
Hannibal, Mo. 1918	61	1:1:1	22.46	5.60	11.0	114.2				8½	2510	4417			
Mobile, Ala. 1919	18	1:1:1	21.90	5.45	11.0	118.9				9		5591		3306	
Interior Rib 1953	5	See Test No. 2					117.3	104.4	11				8125		
Hull just above mean water line 1953	2	See Test No. 2											8787	3050	
Hull below low-water line 1953	3	See Test No. 2											11,204		516
Duplicate Mix 1953	10	1:1:1	20.42	5.5	11.0	108.0	95.0	87.1	9	8	4348	5468			
Suggested Mix for Exposure to Sea Water 1953		1:2.75:2.6		5.5	6.0			85—95		3	2500	3750			

Fig. 12-2. Comparative strength of concrete.

An important recommendation was made to the corporation by Duff Abrams regarding the use of cement in these proposed ships. He recognized that the fineness of cement affected compressive strength and found that the cement should be reground so that 90 percent or more passed a 200-mesh sieve. Figure 12-1 gives average unit weights and average gradations of these lightweight aggregates.

The second vessel to use this expanded lightweight aggregate was the 7,500-ton ship, *Selma*.* Prior to and during use of these lightweight aggregates, a series of test cylinders was made. The results showed a 4,417-psi compressive strength at 28 days. Test cylinders obtained during the construction of the *Selma* gave a compressive strength of 5,591 psi. Diatomaceous earth was added to the lightweight aggregates and cement, the quantity being 1.5 percent by weight. This took the place of present-day pozzolans for extra fines.

Some of the ship's statistics are given:

Displacement . . . . 7,500 tons
Length . . . . 434 feet, 3 inches
Beam . . . . .54 feet
Draft (fully loaded) . . . . .26 feet
Full cargo displacement . . . . .13,000 tons
Propulsion—triple expansion engine . . . . .2,800 h.p.
Speed . . . . 10 1/2 knots

Total concrete used . . . . .2,660 cubic yards
Total reinforcing rods used . . . . .1,500 tons (1,165 pounds per cubic yard)
Total aggregates used . . . . 7,500 tons
Side hull thickness . . . . 4 inches
Bottom hull thickness . . . . 5 inches

The *Selma* was launched in June, 1919, and was put into immediate service transporting crude oil from Tampico to Texas refinery ports. After three years of satisfactory service, the *Selma* ran aground on the South Jetty at Tampico. The stranding cracked the *Selma's* hull towards the bow. No company would guarantee repairs, and the *Selma* was towed out into Galveston Bay, her seacocks were opened and she settled onto the bottom with part of her hull exposed. The *Selma* remains there to this day.

In July, 1953 (34 years later), the Expanded Shale and Clay Institute undertook an investigation into the condition of the *Selma's* concrete after this long exposure of the hull to sea water, tidal action, and salt-laden air. Specimens were taken from the submerged and exposed portions of the hull. Other sections were taken from inside the hull, interior ribs and compartment bulkheads. The condition of the reinforcing rods was excellent, showing no signs of rust except for a light coat that existed when the concrete was poured. The results of these tests and that of a duplicate mix, patterned after the original mix, are given in Fig. 12-2 to show comparative strength of concrete. This duplicate concrete yielded a seven-day strength of 4,348 psi and a 28-day compressive strength of 5,468 psi. This somewhat higher strength reflects the better quality cements of today, plus the decreased weight of the lightweight aggregates. It also reflects the more uniform expansion that is developed in today's expanded shale aggregates.

*Information on this vessel is taken with permission from "Story of the *Selma*," Expanded Shale and Clay Institute, Washington, D. C.

Two series of tests were carried out, the first being on five two-inch cubes cut from an interior rib of the ship, which were found to have an average compressive strength, when correlated to 6 x 12-inch cylinders, of 8,125 psi. Two similar cubes were cut from the hull section just above the mean water line and were found to have an average compressive strength of 10,338 psi, which, when correlated to a 6 x 12-inch cylinder, would indicate 8,787 psi. (A factor of 0.85 has been used in correlating two-inch cubes to 6 x 12-inch cylinders.) Refer to Fig. 12-1 for unit weights, both saturated and dry, and percentages of absorption.

Three months later the second series of tests was conducted with two large sections being cut from the hull from below the low water line and three two-inch cubes sawed from one of these specimens. They were found to have an average compressive strength of 13,181 psi, which, when correlated to the above factor 0.85, indicates a 6 x 12-inch cylinder compressive strength of 11,204 psi. The second specimen taken from below the water line contained a 5/8-inch smooth reinforcing bar with an embedment of 13 inches. A pullout test on this bar was conducted by Professor Sophus Thompson, head of the Civil Engineering Department, Southern Methodist University. Bond failure on this specimen occurred at a load of 13,175 pounds, or 516 psi. In a report on the general condition of the concrete, Professor Thompson states that there was a slight coating of rust on the bars, but no pits or corroded places. He further states that the concrete suffered no apparent damage from exposure.

A separate sample of concrete from the hull was also forwarded to Professor Adrian Pauw of the Civil Engineering Department, University of Missouri, for a test of elastic modulus. Two runs were made, one loading the specimen to about 4,000 psi, and the second run loading the specimen to about 6,000 psi. The secant modulus on the first run calculated 3,100,000 psi, and on the second run, 3,000,000 psi. The permanent deformation was approximately 0.00007 inch per inch for both runs.

BIBLIOGRAPHY

Concrete Topics. Technical Service Dept. Bulletins, Kaiser Permanente & Gypsum Corp., Permanente, Calif.

Permanente Cement Technical Literature, "Cement Types and Uses," Kaiser Cement & Gypsum Corp., Permanente, Calif.

Simplified Concrete Design Using Basalite Expanded Shale Aggregate, Basalt Rock Company, Inc., Napa, California

Guide for Structural Light Weight Aggregate Concrete, ACI Committee 213, American Concrete Institute, Detroit, Michigan.

Perlite Light Weight Insulating Concrete, Catalog 30-1967, Perlite Institute, Inc., New York, N.Y.

Basic Facts About Perlite, No. BF-68, Perlite Institute, Inc., New York, N.Y.

Light Weight Concrete, Information Sheet No. 7, Rev. No. 1, 4-66, Expanded Shale and Clay Institute, Washington, D.C.

Story of the Selma, Expanded Shale and Clay Institute, Washington, D.C.

Celatom for Concrete, Form No. A 561, Eagle-Picher Industries, Inc., Ohio.

Boatbuilding In Your Own Backyard, S. S. Rabl, Cornell Maritime Press, Cambridge, Md.

Concrete Information, Cement and Concrete Association of Australia, Ref. C-39.

J. G. Byrne and W. Wright, "An Investigation of 'Ferro-Cement' Using Expanded Metal, *Concrete and Constructional Engineering,* Vol. LVI, No. 12 (London: December, 1961), pp. 429–433.

L.D.G. Collen and R. W. Kirwan, "Some Notes on the Characteristics of Ferro-Cement, *"Civil Engineering and Public Works Review* (London: February, 1959) pp. 195, 196.

"Tentative Requirements for the Construction of Yachts and Small Craft in Ferro-Cement," Technical Note FC/REQ/1, dated 2 January 1967, Lloyd's Register of Shipping, London EC3, England.

Tensile Testing of Materials, B.S. 18, British Standards Institution.

Specifications for Hot Rolled Bars and Hard Drawn Wire, B.S. 735, Part 1 and Part 2, British Standards Institution.

Curing of Concrete Samples for Compressive Testing, B.S. 1881, British Standards Institution.

"Practices for Mixing, Handling, Compaction and Curing of Concrete, C.P. 114, dated 1957, paragraphs 306–308, British Standards Institution.

"The Use of the Metric System in the Construction Industry," P.D. 6031, dated December, 1968, 2nd edition, British Standards Institution.

Ferro-Cement Times, North American Ferro-Cement Marine Association, Mountain View, California.

Concrete Boatbuilding, G. W. Jackson and W. M. Sutherland; John de Graff, Inc., Tuckahoe, N.Y., 1969.

How to Build a Ferro-Cement Boat, J. Samson and G. Wellens; Samson Marine Design Enterprises Ltd., Ladner, B.C., Canada, 1968.

The Elements of Yacht Design, Norman L. Skene (revised by Francis S. Kinney); Dodd, Mead & Co., New York, N.Y.

INDEX